T0026109

POETRY 101

FROM SHAKESPEARE AND RUPI KAUR TO IAMBIC PENTAMETER AND BLANK VERSE, EVERYTHING YOU NEED TO KNOW ABOUT POETRY

SUSAN DALZELL

Adams Media
New York London Toronto Sydney New Delhi

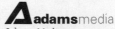

Adams Media
An Imprint of Simon & Schuster, Inc.
100 Technology Center Drive
Stoughton, MA 02072

First Adams Media hardcover edition September 2018

ADAMS MEDIA and colophon are trademarks of Simon & Schuster.

For information about special discounts for bulk purchases, please contact Simon & Schuster Special Sales at 1-866-506-1949 or business@simonandschuster.com.

The Simon & Schuster Speakers Bureau can bring authors to your live event. For more information or to book an event contact the Simon & Schuster Speakers Bureau at 1-866-248-3049 or visit our website at www.simonspeakers.com.

Manufactured in the United States of America

4 2022

Library of Congress Cataloging-in-Publication Data has been applied for.

ISBN 978-1-5072-0839-7
ISBN 978-1-5072-0840-3 (ebook)

Many of the designations used by manufacturers and sellers to distinguish their products are claimed as trademarks. Where those designations appear in this book and Simon & Schuster, Inc., was aware of a trademark claim, the designations have been printed with initial capital letters.

DEDICATION

For Wil and Liam

CONTENTS

INTRODUCTION

Poetry is among the most complex art forms evolved by the human race. It uses words in unique ways to create emotional responses, sometimes using those words in vastly different ways than we do in ordinary speech. It's also one of the oldest art forms; no one really knows when the first poem was composed—just that it was thousands of years ago.

Maybe you've read poetry your whole life; maybe you're coming to it for the first time; maybe you just want to learn something about it; or maybe you have an urge to start scribbling verses yourself. No matter which of these applies to you, you'll find something of value in this book.

Poetry 101 doesn't make any assumptions about what you know or what you may have been taught back in the day. Instead you will find help in exploring what poetry can mean in your own life. You'll learn or review the basic terms and vocabulary of poetry. You'll get an overview of the history of poetry and the cultures from which poets have emerged. You'll learn the life stories of some of the greatest poets in the English language and why those poets' works are so highly regarded. You'll learn more about the topics poets have been drawn to write about and compare and contrast how different poets approach similar themes. You'll look at works by the poets of ancient Greece, the European Middle Ages, Victorian England, and onward to the Internet-fueled poets of today.

Sometimes poetry is formal, following strict rules of language and form. Sometimes it's wild and loose; you know this if you've ever attended a poetry reading. Poetry can express love and hate and joy and grief and anger and confusion and humor. Sometimes it is easy to understand—"Eeny meeny miny mo, catch a tiger by the toe"—but sometimes it's so dense and tricky you can read it three, four, five, sixty times and still struggle to interpret its meaning. That's another way in which *Poetry 101* can give you a hand. Whether you choose to read this book cover to cover or to dive in and out of its many sections, it will help you form a working definition of poetry that makes sense to you. Hopefully, reading this book will encourage you to seek out poems themselves. Read them. Memorize them. Speak them out loud. Share them with your friends, companions, or children. Find poems that speak to you and savor them. Maybe even try writing some verses yourself.

Doing any of these things will increase your enjoyment of this art form. No matter your poetry background or how you hope to use poetry in the future, *Poetry 101* has you covered. Now let's delve into the history and theory of poetry!

HOW TO READ A POEM

Push Through the Fear

Whether we want to admit it or not, it can be scary—or at least daunting—to face a page on which a few words have been arranged into something called a poem. We know where we stand with sentences and paragraphs, but everything can feel a bit wobbly when words are shaped into other, less familiar, forms and patterns. It seems hard to know where to start. In the next section, we'll take a closer look at the techniques of meter and rhythm. For now, here are a few ideas to help in your approach to a new poem.

USE YOUR VOICE

With few exceptions, poems are meant to be spoken. The human voice breathes both life and meaning into the words. A poem that is difficult to understand on paper may start to make a lot more sense once you read it out loud. Sentences that appear disjointed, thanks to breaks on the page, may piece together smoothly when heard by your ear.

Play with the speed that you speak: does slowing down or speeding up help you hear the rhymes more easily? Maybe you can't hear any rhymes, but reciting a string of words that all start with the same letter sounds good. Do you find yourself falling into a rhythm as you speak, emphasizing certain words or syllables? Does the poem sound better if you pause at the end of each line, or carry on until you reach the end of a sentence?

READ CLOSELY

Don't skip stuff. Read the poem from beginning to end, even if it's slow going. Take your time and don't rush. Poetry can be dense, with layers of meaning that may not be revealed on a first read.

Read with a pencil in hand. (Or a pen, if you're brave.) Writing your thoughts down really helps you engage with the poem. Underline words. Circle them. Jot down questions in the margin. Put an asterisk next to a line you really like or a question mark next to one that makes no sense. Mark where the sentences finish.

Factors to Consider

- *The Title.* Start with the poem's title. Some titles give an accurate preview of the poem's subject but others possess a less obvious meaning. Keep the title in mind as you read through the poem.
- *The Poet's Name.* If you recognize his or her name, take a second to think about what you know about him or her. Did you like his other poems? Does she write in a formal or informal style?
- *The Poem's Appearance.* Observe how the poem looks on the page. Are there many breaks? Does the poet use a lot of white space or do the words crash into one another?
- *Context.* A poem isn't written in a vacuum. While some poems hold clear meanings on their own, others gain more power when applying external factors. Was the poem written during wartime? Was the poet a member of a minority group? Did he or she write in secret? Or for a large audience?
- *The Speaker.* Who is the speaker? Even if the poem is written in first person, the speaker isn't necessarily the poet. Many poets use a persona—an imaginary identity—to write. Can you imagine the speaker in real life?

- *Tone*. What is the attitude of the poem? Is it lighthearted and humorous? Does it drip with sarcasm? Or angst?
- *Patterns and Symbols*. Look for patterns. Are there sounds, words, or lines that repeat? Does the poem circle back on itself at any point? Are there repeating motifs or symbols?
- *Vocabulary*. If you encounter a word you don't recognize, don't move on. Remember: every single word counts in a poem. Take a moment to look up the word's definition. If it has several potential meanings, consider which one fits best within the poem's context.

One way to understand a poem's meaning is to strip it down to the essentials. If the language is flowery, take away the adjectives. If there are metaphors or figurative language, translate the phrases into plain language. Paraphrase the poem to reveal a basic plot or point. Then use that as a framework to build the poem back into shape again, adding layers of language until it returns to the form in which the poet presented it. A paraphrased poem, after all, is not a poem. Read it again, and you may find that parts of the poem now spring to life in ways they didn't on your initial read.

Memorizing Poetry

Want to really get to know a poem? Memorize it. If that sounds old-fashioned, it is. For centuries, schoolchildren have memorized poems by Chaucer, Shakespeare, and Edgar Allan Poe, to name a few popular choices. Memorizing a poem creates intimacy between the words and you, an understanding that drills deeper into your mind than simply reading the words. Even better, it means you carry the poem with you wherever you go.

STANZA, METER, AND FORM

The Scaffolding Holding Poems Together

Quite often, the beauty in a poem is the result of careful scaffolding put in place by the poet. The thoughts may be original, but most poets use tried-and-true poetry tools and techniques to create a compelling poem. A skilled poet takes a familiar form, say a sonnet, and transforms it into a breathtakingly original piece of art. Even Modern poetry uses many hidden and not-so-hidden poetic devices to cast a spell on readers.

STANZA

Stanzas are to poetry what paragraphs are to prose. Essentially, a stanza is a grouping of lines. Typically, a poem is composed of multiple stanzas. They might all have the same number of lines, but that won't necessarily be the case.

Common Stanza Types

Couplet: Two lines of verse grouped together, usually rhyming.

Terza rima: Three lines of verse grouped together, with an interlocking rhyme pattern of *aba, bcb, cdc, ded*, and so forth. The poem concludes with a two-line stanza that rhymes with the middle line of the second-to-last stanza. It's an Italian form first used in English by Geoffrey Chaucer.

Quatrains: Four lines of verse grouped together. The rhyme pattern can vary, but often follows a pattern of *aaaa, aabb, abab*. Sometimes *quatrain* refers to a poem with only four lines.

Cinquains: (pronounced *sing-KEYN*) Five lines of verse grouped together. Rhyme patterns vary.

Adelaide Crapsey

Adelaide Crapsey (1878–1914) is an American poet credited with inventing the cinquain poem, a twenty-two syllable, five-line poem. She died of tuberculosis in 1914 when she was only thirty-six years old. Her first book of poetry, *Verse*, was published a year later and included twenty-eight cinquains. *Verse* sold very well in the 1920s and 1930s and again later in the century and inspired many other poets, including Carl Sandburg.

METER, RHYTHM, AND FEET

Meter and rhythm, rhythm and meter—the two are intricately linked in poetry. Think of it this way: rhythm is the stressed and unstressed syllables that happen when we speak and meter is the pattern created by those syllables. Let's break it down one more level: a foot is a unit of rhythm. String the feet together in a pattern and you form a meter.

There are five basic kinds of feet:

1. Iamb (Unaccented-Accented)
2. Trochee (Accented-Unaccented)
3. Spondee (Accented-Accented)
4. Anapest (Unaccented-Unaccented-Accented)
5. Dactyl (Accented-Unaccented-Unaccented)

To form a poem, we need to make it a little more complicated. As we know, poems are composed of lines. Meter can be identified by the number of feet per line. Take iambs, for example. An iambic dimeter poem has two iambs per line; an iambic trimeter poem has three iambs per line; and so forth.

The most recognizable meter is iambic pentameter, which has five iambs per line. Poets love to write in iambic pentameter. Shakespeare used iambic pentameter when he wrote in verse for his plays and almost exclusively for his sonnets:

"Shall I / compare / thee to / a sum / mer's day?
Thou art / more love / ly and / more tem / per ate."

—"Sonnet 18," William Shakespeare

For another example, let's look at the rarer trochaic meters. American poet Henry Wadsworth Longfellow famously used a trochaic tetrameter—four trochee feet per line—in 1855 for his epic poem *The Song of Hiawatha*:

"By the / shore of / Git che / Gu mee,
By the / shi ning / Big-Sea -Wat er,
At the / door way / of his / wig wam,
In the / pleas ant / sum mer / morn ing,
Hi a / wath a / stood and / wait ed."

—*The Song of Hiawatha*, Henry Wadsworth Longfellow

Although a poem may be identified as using a certain meter, poets often play with the meter within a poem. A poem following only the strictest of rhythms gets boring fast. While a poet would struggle to use a spondaic meter for an entire poem, dropping in an occasional spondee foot helps to add emphasis and variety. To familiarize yourself with the mechanics of a poem, try scanning it.

How to Scan a Poem

- Read the poem out loud. Listen carefully to which syllables you naturally emphasize.
- Mark above the stressed syllables with an accent.
- Mark above the unstressed syllables with a breve. (It looks like a tiny squashed u.)
- Break the syllables into feet, using slashes between the words or between the syllables within a word, if necessary. Identify the feet (iamb, trochee, spondee, anapest, or dactyl).
- Count the number of feet per line (1 = monometer, 2 = dimeter, 3 = trimeter, 4 = tetrameter, 5 = pentameter, 6 = hexameter, 7 = heptameter or septenary, 8 = octameter).
- Combine the foot with the (average) number per line and you've identified the poem's meter. For example, a poem that scans with five unstressed/stressed iamb feet per line is written in iambic pentameter.
- Learning to scan can be difficult. Take your time and be patient. If you aren't discovering a pattern, try saying the poem out loud again and listen for whether some accents are heavier than others.

POETIC FORMS

Poems come in many shapes, sizes, and styles. They can be brief: a haiku is only three lines, traditionally following a five-seven-five syllable format. Limericks convey humor in just five lines, following a rhyme pattern of *aabba*. Poems also can be incredibly lengthy: ballads sometimes stretch into hundreds of lines. Poetic forms may be defined by appearance: concrete poems (also called pattern or shape poems) are written so they form the shape of an object on the page—a concrete poem about a Christmas tree looks like a Christmas tree. Other forms rely on a strict format: a pantoum consists of four-line stanzas where the second and fourth lines of each stanza are repeated as the first and third lines of the next stanza.

Throughout this book, as we look at specific poets, topics, and historical periods, we'll define and examine poetic forms. Some poets are closely associated with a form they favor. Some topics, especially love and death, are interpreted again and again using the same forms, such as sonnets and elegies. Historically, the popularity of certain genres of poetry has ebbed and flowed when public tastes changed. Lists naming specific poetry forms can stretch into the fifties, but it's important to note that poetic forms are limited only by the creativity of poets. Forms are always evolving as poets adapt language to suit their purposes.

ANCIENT GREEKS AND ROMANS

Finding Our Poetic Roots

The Greeks and Romans may have been great warriors, but they were also great poets. Their poetry has stood the test of time, providing structure, themes, and plots that continue to resonate today.

THE GREEKS

The earliest written Greek poems date back to the eighth century B.C.E., but scholars believe the Greeks were composing and reciting poetry via an oral tradition for centuries before then. Even once they invented an alphabet and began recording their poems for posterity, the Greeks continued to enjoy their poems primarily as performance pieces. Poets recited poems accompanied by the lyre, sometimes alongside dancers, before audiences both big and small.

Epic Poetry

Historians credit the Greeks with inventing the epic poem, a genre that serves as a cornerstone of Western literature. An epic poem tells a long, grand, and detailed history of a people and their culture, featuring a hero and his adventures. Epic poems originally were shared orally and could be adapted by the poet to suit the situation or audience. Epic poetry is written in dactylic hexameter, meaning each line has six metrical feet. The first five can be either a dactyl (Accented-Unaccented-Unaccented) or a spondee (Accented-Accented) and the final foot is always a spondee. This meter is well suited to speech and has just enough built-in rhythmic flexibility to make a long recitation less tedious.

Sometime between the twelfth and eighth centuries B.C.E., a Greek poet named Homer composed the epic poems *The Iliad* and *The Odyssey*, considered the oldest complete works of Western literature. Not much is known about Homer—so little, in fact, that some theorists think works credited to him may have been composed by several poets. Texts often refer to him as blind, based on an assumption that he based the blind minstrel character of Demodokos, in *The Odyssey*, on himself. *The Iliad* takes place during the final year of the Trojan War while the Greeks were laying siege to Troy, and features the hero and warrior Achilles. (The poem takes its name from Ilium, the Greek name for Troy.) *The Odyssey* takes place after the Trojan War, and relates the hero Odysseus's epic ten-year journey to return to his kingdom. Homer used language rich with simile and metaphor and adopted dactylic hexameter, setting a precedent for epic poetry followed today. For centuries, writers have told and retold the stories within these two poems. We continue to be fascinated by their characters and plots.

Common Characteristics of Epic Poems

- Opens with the poet asking a muse for help
- Written in dactylic hexameter
- Tells a historic tale that takes place over many years
- Central hero possesses superhuman powers, including great courage
- Supernatural or divine powers intervene and meddle with humans
- Long length comparable to that of a novel

Historians believe Hesiod, a Greek poet and farmer, lived a few years after Homer. Hesiod's poems were didactic, meaning they were intended to teach a lesson. Like Homer, he composed using dactylic hexameter. Three of his complete works have survived: *The Shield of Heracles*, *Works and Days*, and *Theogony*. *Works and Days*, written about 700 B.C.E., is an epic poem told from a farmer's point of view and includes myths, legends, and moral teachings on the value of hard work. Hesiod used an authorial "I" as narrator, a first in European literature. In *Theogony*, Hesiod tells the stories of the Greek gods, from the creation of the world onward, and their epic interactions. Hesiod was retelling and synthesizing mythic stories from throughout Greece, but his versions became the most popular.

Lyric Poetry

Lyric poetry emerged in Greece by the seventh century B.C.E. Greek tastes shifted away from the lengthy heroic tales of the epic poets to briefer, more personal, lyric poems. Lyrics are the kind of poem recited by poets at weddings. Lyric poets experimented with the form, trying new meters and rhyming patterns. The term *lyric* is derived from *lyre*, which provides a clue to the form's musical roots. Lyric poems in Greece were sung and expressed emotion, not unlike today's pop songs.

Sappho is the most famous of the lyric poets and is one of the few female poets of the ancient era whose work is still remembered. Born on the island of Lesbos sometime within 630–610 B.C.E., most likely to a wealthy family, she was well known in her own time. The ancient Library of Alexandria collected and housed nine volumes of her poetry, but all were lost when the library later burned down. Much of her reputation is based on quotations by others. Sappho's only surviving complete poem is the twenty-eight-line "Hymn to Aphrodite," although portions of a few others have survived. She wrote concisely and clearly in an Aeolic Greek dialect, but with passion, about love, infatuation, and romantic desire for both males and females. Although historically often characterized as a lesbian—the term *sapphic* refers to female homosexuality—her personal sexuality is unknown.

Sapphic Meter

Attributed first to Sappho, this meter consists of three lines of eleven syllables and a final line of five syllables. The four-line stanzas can be repeated any number of times.

Contemporaries of the Greek poet Pindar, who was born in the sixth century B.C.E. and died in the fifth century B.C.E., considered him one of the greatest lyric poets of his time. About 25 percent of his complete poems survived antiquity and most are epinicion—choral victory odes that honor winners in war or athletics. An aristocrat himself, Pindar received commissions to write poems for special occasions for much of his nearly fifty-year career, including odes for the Olympics. His poems praised the gods, retold myths, and provided moral guidance on the dangers of excessive pride. He experimented throughout his career with meter and rarely repeated a style. His work contains many references well known to his contemporary audiences, but for modern readers their obscurity makes his poems difficult to read and interpret.

THE ROMANS

Roman poetry, written in Latin, borrowed much in form and style from the Greeks. Although the forms are familiar, the Romans produced their own crop of talented and prolific lyric, epic, and elegiac poets who produced work that stands in quality shoulder-to-shoulder with that of their Greek counterparts. The work of many of these poets, including Virgil and Ovid, continues to be revered today.

Virgil, born Publius Vergilius Maro in 70 B.C.E., is one of the greatest ancient Roman poets. He wrote pastoral and didactic poems, but he is best known for his epic poem, *The Aeneid*, commissioned by Emperor Augustus to glorify Rome. Virgil modeled it after Homer's epic poems, telling the story of Aeneas, a hero of the Trojan war whose descendants founded Rome. *The Aeneid*, due to the language's beauty and Virgil's skills as a storyteller, was widely considered a literary masterpiece from the point of its publication, shortly after Virgil's death.

Ovid, Horace, and Catullus join Virgil in status as revered Latin-language poets. Ovid, born in 43 B.C.E., composed *Metamorphoses*, an epic poem in Greek style that begins with creation and tells the stories of Greek and Roman gods on through to the deification of Julius Caesar. Horace was a Roman poet, born in 65 B.C.E., known both for his lyric *Odes*, which celebrate friendship and love, and for *Ars Poetica*, a poem written as a letter to a Roman senator and his son providing advice to young poets. Catullus, born around 84 B.C.E., was an innovative lyric poet, credited with developing several literary techniques including alliteration, the repetition of initial consonant sounds in adjacent words. Many of his poems expressed love for a married woman called Lesbia.

THE ANGLO-SAXONS

How the English Became the English

The Roman Empire extended far beyond Italy. At its peak, Roman troops had helped expand Roman rule to northern Africa, much of the Middle East, and most of what we now consider Europe. Julius Caesar had tried to expand the empire to include Britain, but his attempts in 55 and 54 B.C.E. were thwarted by strong resistance and a revolt in Gaul, which caused him to withdraw. In 43 C.E., under the direction of Emperor Claudius, the Romans successfully invaded Britain. They would spend the next forty years pushing deeper into the isles, defeating the Britons and Caledonians as far north as the Moray Firth in 84 C.E. at the Battle of Mons Graupius. But over the next several centuries, as the Roman Empire faced threats on all its borders, troop numbers in Britain were reduced. By the middle of the fourth century, Britain also faced many attacks from tribal groups, including the native Picts and Scots from the north and Germanic tribes from Angeln and Saxony. Roman soldiers struggled to meet the threats. By 410 C.E., Rome had determined that Britain was no longer a priority. They severed their claim to Britain, and recalled all Romans left in Britain back to Rome. It was too little, too late for Rome: that same year Rome itself was sacked by the Visigoths.

With the Romans gone, Britain was in a state of change. The invading tribes, including Germanic Angles and Saxons and Danish Jutes and Frisians, began settling in large numbers and putting down roots of their own in what are now England and Wales. The new residents spoke different languages and were largely illiterate: Roman ways were quickly forgotten. The Anglo-Saxon period began, lasting from 410 until William the Conqueror invaded in 1066.

ANGLO-SAXON POETRY

The new era brought a new language—Old English—emerging as a synthesis of the West Germanic dialects and Latin, spread by missionaries after the arrival of St. Augustine in 597. The missionaries also spread the use of Roman letters for a written language. With literacy came literature. The oldest surviving text of Old English literature is a poem written by the seventh-century poet Caedmon, who is often called the "father of English poetry." Sometime between 658 and 680, Caedmon composed a nine-line poem titled "Caedmon's Hymn." In the poem, Caedmon—a shepherd who later became a monk—praises God as the creator of man. The names of very few other Anglo-Saxon poets are known and only four—Caedmon, Cynewulf, Bede, and King Alfred—have work that can still be read today.

Scop

An Anglo-Saxon poet was called a scop (pronounced *shop*). He recited memorized poetry while playing a harp or a lyre. Some scops were affiliated with royal or noble courts and others may have traveled, performing in village halls.

Scholars believe poetry as an oral tradition was widespread among the Anglo-Saxons. The sophistication and shared style of the written poems that have survived indicate a rich tradition that would have developed only through the contributions of many poets. Roughly 400 of the surviving Anglo-Saxon manuscripts were written in Old English. For poetry, the four major codices, or books, are: the Junius Manuscript, an illustrated compilation of biblical narratives; the Exeter Book, an anthology stored at Exeter Cathedral since the eleventh century; the Vercelli Book, which includes poetry and prose; and the Nowell Codex, which contains the only copy of the poem *Beowulf*, as well as other prose and poetry. The poems generally are either religious poems or epic poems about a hero, but there are also elegy poems of mourning and even riddle poems.

ANGLO-SAXON POETIC STYLE

Alliteration and Stress: Anglo-Saxon poems were composed primarily for recitation. To make them easier to memorize, they tended to be highly rhythmic and used a form of alliteration, rather than meter and rhyme, to achieve that rhythm. (Alliteration repeats the initial consonant sound of a word.) In Anglo-Saxon poetry, a line has four stressed syllables with a pause, called a caesura, in the middle. The alliteration always carries across the pause, with the first stressed syllable after the pause alliterating with one or both stressed syllables in the first half of the line. The resulting poetry when recited can sound almost like a chant, harsher in tone than Greek and Latin poetry.

Kenning: Instead of metaphors or similes, Old English poems used kennings. A kenning is a description of a noun using a two-word phrase, such as battle-sweat for blood or slaughter-storm for battle. Kennings were also frequently used in Old Norse poetry.

BEOWULF

Beowulf is the best known of the surviving Anglo-Saxon poems. An anonymous poet first wrote *Beowulf*, an epic poem, by around 800. The surviving manuscript, however, was written closer to the eleventh century. *Beowulf* tells a bloody and violent story in 3,200 lines. The sixth-century hero, Beowulf, battles against three monsters. The first, Grendel, has kept the castle of the Danish king Hrothgar under siege for twelve years. Beowulf rips off Grendel's arm, and the creature bleeds to death. Next, Beowulf battles Grendel's mother and slays her with a magic sword. Finally, fifty years later, when Beowulf is the king of the Geats, he must defend his own people from a dragon. This battle is his last: both he and the dragon die.

Beowulf is based on an older Scandinavian tale passed down orally. Although its roots are in pagan stories, it includes many Christian themes inserted by the poet. The plot is supplemented by digressions on other historical events, creating a rich, complex narrative. Although the poem is widely studied today, and is often credited as the first major work in the canon of English literature, it was kept in obscurity until the nineteenth and twentieth centuries, when it was rediscovered by critics and writers.

"LO, praise of the prowess of people-kings
of spear-armed Danes, in days long sped,
we have heard, and what honor the athelings won!"

—*Beowulf* (Francis B. Gummere translation), Anonymous

GEOFFREY CHAUCER (CA. 1340–1400)

The Father of English Literature

What does it take to be considered the Father of English Literature? For Geoffrey Chaucer, it meant writing in the common man's language, English, and doing so in such an artful way that his work has never really gone out of style. Not a bad feat for a man who took his last breath in 1400. Chaucer is a poet for the ages, a man whose body of work encompasses not only poems, but story collections, translations, and scientific treatises. And all this while living a life of incredible upward mobility, in an age when most people were stuck in the social class they were born into.

THE SOCIAL CLIMBER

Chaucer was born in London to John Chaucer and Agnes de Copton in or near 1340. His middle-class family had gained their wealth from working as wine merchants. Chaucer's father may have been the deputy to the king's butler. It was that connection, most likely, that led to the teenage Chaucer serving in the court of Countess Elizabeth of Ulster, the Duke of Clarence's wife. In 1359, he set off to fight in the Hundred Years' War in France, was captured, and then was ransomed by King Edward III. He married well, in 1366, to Philippa de Roet, a lady-in-waiting to the queen. (Her sister, Katherine Swynford, was the third wife of John of Gaunt, the king's son.) Chaucer spent most of his life in royal service, acting as a diplomat throughout France, Spain, and Italy, where he was introduced to the writing of Dante, Petrarch, and Boccaccio. In England, he also held a series of government appointments, even serving as the representative of Kent in the House of Commons. He was well paid for his work, and he and Philippa received royal stipends.

After Philippa died in 1387, Chaucer lost the income from her royal annuities. He continued to work, but his last few years were ones of financial hardship. He died on October 25, 1400, and was buried on the grounds of Westminster Abbey. The part of the Abbey where he lies is now called Poets' Corner and is the final resting place for nearly thirty other poets, a tradition begun in the late sixteenth century.

A GIFTED POET

Chaucer was fluent in Latin, French, and Italian. So why did he choose to write in English? In fifteenth-century England, poetry was typically composed in either Latin or French, the language spoken by the nobility. Chaucer's English—Middle English—was widespread among commoners, but wasn't a language used for literature. Chaucer's bold choice—whatever his reasons—ushered in an era where writing in the vernacular, or common language, became acceptable in literature.

Chaucer wrote several dream-vision poems early in his career, most notably *The Book of the Duchess*, *The Parliament of Fowls*, and *The House of Fame*. He was likely influenced by a thirteenth-century French dream narrative, *Roman de la Rose*. These poems, popular in the Middle Ages, used a dream sequence framework to bookend the main narrative. The poet, or dreamer, related a fantastical experience, usually while escorted by a wise guide. In Chaucer's case, he liked to depict his narrator falling asleep while reading a book, which then inspires the contents of the dream. Chaucer's subject matter for these poems was wide ranging, covering courtly love, bereavement, and fame.

Italian poetry inspired Chaucer when he penned the narrative poem *Troilus and Criseyde* (ca. 1382). His basic plot of doomed lovers during the Trojan War was borrowed from Boccaccio. The poem is notable for its seven-line iambic pentameter stanzas, called rime (rhyme) royal, following a rhyming scheme of *ababbcc*. Chaucer was among the first English poets to use the meter, a practice widely imitated by others, including Shakespeare and John Milton.

"And specially, from every shires ende
Of Engelond to Caunterbury they wende,
The holy blisful martir for to seke,
That hem hath holpen, whan that they were seke."

—"Prologue," *The Canterbury Tales*, Geoffrey Chaucer

The Canterbury Tales

The Canterbury Tales (ca. 1380s) is Chaucer's most famous, and praised, work. It is written in iambic pentameter with rhyming couplets, in which every two lines rhyme with each other. The meter also is called heroic couplet. Chaucer never finished this ambitious story collection, completing only twenty-four of his planned 120 stories.

He framed the stories by introducing thirty pilgrims traveling together from London to Canterbury Cathedral. To pass the time, their innkeeper host asked each pilgrim to tell four stories—two on the way and two on the return. The pilgrims represent a wide cross section of society, including a knight, a squire, and a yeoman; a prioress, a monk, and a friar; a merchant; a clerk of Oxford; a miller; a reeve (that is, someone who supervised the farming of land); and a wife of Bath, among others. By letting the characters tell their stories, Chaucer was free to write in different styles and voices. "The Miller's Tale," for example, includes fart jokes and risqué humor, while "The Knight's Tale" sticks to themes of courtly love.

There is no one, definitive original *Canterbury Tales*. The surviving manuscripts—eighty-three of them—were probably not copied during Chaucer's lifetime. They contain many versions that shuffle the order of the tales and leave out or include different fragments of text, which alters the transitions between tales, and even change the narrators, leaving generations of scholars with plenty of material to debate and critique. Regardless, the editions printed and circulated today are met by modern readers who may be as amused and moved by the stories as medieval readers were.

CHRISTOPHER MARLOWE (1564–1593)

The Poet Who Inspired Shakespeare

Born in 1564, Christopher Marlowe was a contemporary of William Shakespeare. His life was short—he was murdered in 1593 when he was only twenty-nine—but his influence on English poetry, literature, and drama was profound.

Marlowe was born in Canterbury, the eldest son of shoemaker John Marlowe, and attended the King's School, Canterbury. He showed his intelligence from a young age: Corpus Christi College at the University of Cambridge awarded him a scholarship. The university granted him a bachelor of arts in 1584 and he qualified to continue for a master's degree. When it came time to grant him that degree, though, university officials hesitated. Marlowe had been absent from Cambridge for long periods, more than allowed, and officials were concerned about where he had spent his excursions. Rumors flew that perhaps he was in France training to become a Roman Catholic priest.

It took members of Queen Elizabeth's Privy Council sending a letter declaring he had been away "on matters touching the benefit of his country" to convince them to award the degree. The letter implies he may have been doing spy work on the behalf of her Majesty, Queen Elizabeth, although whether he truly was a spy or not has never been satisfyingly confirmed or refuted. Regardless, Marlowe soon moved to London and embarked on his writing career.

MARLOWE THE POET

Early in his career, while still a student, Marlowe translated verse by the Roman poets Ovid and Lucan. He translated the first book of Lucan's *Pharsalia* and Ovid's *Amores*, one of Ovid's greatest works, from Latin into English. The original *Amores* consisted of forty-nine lyric elegies about an intense love affair between the poet narrator and Corinna, a married woman. Sixteenth-century England was not as open as Roman audiences to steamy poetry: in 1599, Marlowe's *Amores* was banned and publicly burned as offensive.

Ovid wrote using elegiac couplets, with alternating lines of dactylic hexameter and dactylic pentameter. Marlowe's translation used rhymed pentameter couplets. Marlowe's style was more direct and less polished than Ovid's; his translations of both Ovid and Lucan are not regarded as his best work. However, they provided him with excellent training for his later, widely acclaimed, verse.

Blank Verse

Christopher Marlowe was among the first in England to adopt the use of blank verse for his poetry and plays. Blank verse is unrhymed iambic pentameter, introduced in the sixteenth century by Italian poets translating unrhymed Greek and Latin heroic poems. The ten-syllable lines lend themselves well to speech, making this poetic form one of the most popular for playwrights.

Marlowe's lyric poem "The Passionate Shepherd to His Love" was written in iambic tetrameter with a regular rhythm and beat. Published after his death, it was probably written a few years before he died. It is a pastoral poem, meaning it is set in an idealized version of the countryside. Only twenty-four lines long, it consists of a shepherd beseeching a young woman to come and be his wife, tempting her with vivid descriptions of the rural landscape and the surprising wealthy trappings—for a shepherd's wife at least—of her clothing. It's a romantic and pretty poem, well loved and enjoyed by many for centuries, although it's a bit too sweet for some critics.

Marlowe is also well known for writing *Hero and Leander*, based on a poem by Musaeus, a fourth- or fifth-century Greek poet. It tells a Greek myth about doomed lovers: Hero, a priestess of Aphrodite, and Leander, a young man who would swim each night to see her. Despite the tragic ending, Marlowe used wit and comedy to tell their story. Although the poem was unfinished at the time of his death, many consider it one of the finest narrative poems of its time. The poet George Chapman finished the poem and published it in 1598.

"Come live with me and be my love,
And we will all the pleasures prove
That valleys, groves, hills, and fields,
Woods, or steepy mountain yields."

—"The Passionate Shepherd to His Love," Christopher Marlowe

MARLOWE THE PLAYWRIGHT

Marlowe and William Shakespeare were rival playwrights, and quite possibly, also friends. For the sixteenth century, Marlowe is considered second only to Shakespeare in his skills as a dramatist. Marlowe penned only four major plays, written between 1587 and 1593: *Tamburlaine the Great*, *The Jew of Malta*, *The Tragical History of the*

Life and Death of Doctor Faustus, and *Edward II*. *Doctor Faustus* is widely considered a masterpiece, both for its skilled use of iambic pentameter verse and for its intense, tragic drama. Other plays attributed to Marlowe are *Dido, Queen of Carthage*, and *The Massacre at Paris*. Although they were the same age, Marlowe's theatrical career was slightly ahead of Shakespeare's, and his work served as inspiration for the latter. There are schools of thought—never proven—that Marlowe is the true author of some of Shakespeare's plays.

AN UNTIMELY END

Controversy chased Marlowe for much of his short life. In 1589, he and the poet Thomas Watson were charged with homicide and thrown in prison. Marlowe was released after two weeks and Watson after five months, after pleading self-defense. In 1593, the playwright Thomas Kyd accused Marlowe of heresy and blasphemy, after a government raid of Kyd's home found Marlowe's incriminating papers mixed up with Kyd's papers. Instead of jail, Marlowe was required to report to the Privy Council daily. Although he denied it, rumors of atheism—a serious crime—swirled around him and were not resolved before his death.

In 1593, Marlowe met a few friends for a day of dining and conversation at an inn in southeast London. He became involved in a knife fight, possibly over the bill, which ended with one of the men fatally stabbing Marlowe above his eye. The circumstances of his death have led to much speculation over the years, with theories that his murder was not simply a drunken brawl but was connected to his work as a spy. Given his creative output during the short years he was alive, it's a shame that he never evolved into a mature poet; who knows what sort of works he might have penned later in life.

WILLIAM SHAKESPEARE (1564–1616)

A Poet for the Ages

If you know only one poet in the English language, that poet should be William Shakespeare. No other individual wordsmith has influenced Western culture so profoundly. Shakespeare, a sixteenth-century poet and playwright, possessed an amazing command of language. He was talented and prolific: he wrote more than 150 poems and at least thirty-eight plays.

Shakespeare was born in Stratford-upon-Avon in 1564 to John Shakespeare and Mary Arden. His father was a merchant and local politician. Young Shakespeare probably attended the local King's New School in Stratford. He did not attend a university. When he was eighteen, he married Anne Hathaway, pregnant with their first child, Susanna. Two years later, she gave birth to twins, Hamnet and Judith.

There are a lot of holes in Shakespeare's biography. His exact whereabouts for the years between 1585 and 1592 are unknown, although he probably spent the time working as an actor and playwright in London. In the early 1590s, he began composing a collection of sonnets, an endeavor occupying him for roughly six or seven years. He was also busy writing plays, some staged before an outbreak of plague closed all the London theaters from June 1592 to April 1594. During this time, Shakespeare sought and found a wealthy patron, Henry Wriothesley, third Earl of Southampton, who supported him as he wrote the epic, book-length poem *Venus and Adonis* (1593) and the narrative poem *The Rape of Lucrece* (1594). By the time the theaters reopened, he had gained legitimacy as a writer of poetry, an art form more respected and revered in Elizabethan England than drama.

THE SONNETS

Shakespeare did not introduce the sonnet to England—that task was fulfilled by Sir Thomas Wyatt and Henry Howard, Earl of Surrey, in the early sixteenth century—but it is the poetic form most closely associated with him. The first edition of his 154 sonnets was published in 1609, although versions of the sonnets circulated privately for years. Surprisingly, given how beloved these poems have grown over time, they were not as commercially successful during his lifetime as his earlier narrative poems.

Shakespeare's sonnets are divided into two main groups:

- Sonnets 1–126: Addressed to a young man.
- Sonnets 127–154: Addressed to the "dark lady," a mysterious mistress.

The primary theme of the sonnets is love but in Shakespeare's capable hands, that theme encompasses not only romantic love, but death, sex, politics, beauty, and time. His sonnets richly and deftly trace the human experience, spinning the intensely personal experience of one man's love for another man or woman into something recognizable and relatable to us all. The poems are of varying quality but some are breathtaking in their beauty. He left us with so many memorable turns of phrase, such as "Shall I compare thee to a summer's day?" in "Sonnet 18" or "That time of year thou mayst in me behold" in "Sonnet 73." Whether the poems are autobiographical or works of fiction is a subject of much debate.

SONNET TYPES

The simplest definition of a sonnet is a fourteen-line poem in iambic pentameter, with a variable rhyme scheme. But there are many variations. Here are a few of the most common:

Petrarchan Sonnet
Structure: Section one (octave) is eight lines, rhyming *abbaabba*; section two (sestet) is six lines, which can follow a variety of rhyme schemes, including *cdcdcd* or *cdeede*.
Quirks: A turn, or volta, occurs in the ninth line. It introduces a new idea into the poem's narrative or argument.

Italian Sonnet
Structure: Section one is eight lines, rhyming *abbaabba*; section two is six lines, rhyming *cddcee*.
Quirks: An English variation on the Petrarchan sonnet.

Spenserian Sonnet
Structure: Three interlocking quatrains, rhyming *abab bcbc cdcd*, followed by a couplet, *ee*.
Quirks: Devised by poet Edmund Spenser (ca. 1552–1599), the repeated rhymes in this form of sonnet make it difficult to write.

Shakespearean Sonnet
Structure: Section one is four lines, rhyming *abab*; section two is four lines, rhyming *cdcd*; section three is four lines, rhyming *efef*; and section four is a couplet, rhyming *gg*.

Quirks: Sometimes called an English sonnet. The volta isn't always on the ninth line. Shakespeare sometimes waited until the final couplet to make a turn, an innovative practice at the time.

OTHER POEMS

The epic poem *Venus and Adonis* became Shakespeare's most widely printed work during his lifetime. He drew on Ovid's epic narrative poem *Metamorphoses* to tell the story of the goddess Venus and her unrequited love for the human hunter Adonis. Shakespeare's version uses comedy in ways Ovid's did not, shifting Venus from a goddess who wins the love of Adonis to one who can't get the man to shift his attention away from his passion for hunting. He wrote it using a meter of iambic pentameter, each stanza consisting of a quatrain and a couplet, following the rhyme scheme of *ababcc*. (The meter is now named for the poem.) In *The Rape of Lucrece*, Shakespeare composed in rime royal, following Chaucer's example in *Troilus and Criseyde*. For the plot, Shakespeare again drew on classical mythology to tell the Roman story of the nobleman Tarquin, who rapes his friend's wife, Lucrece. The poem raises many complex moral dilemmas, an early representation of Shakespeare's ability to portray intense emotions for his characters.

THE PLAYS

Shakespeare participated actively in the London theater scene. He was a member, as an actor and playwright, of the Lord Chamberlain's Men, one of the city's two leading companies of actors.

They performed both at court for nobility, and at several theaters in London, including the Globe on the Thames's south bank, for commoners. He wrote primarily three types of plays: comedies, such as *A Midsummer Night's Dream* and *All's Well That Ends Well*; tragedies, such as *Hamlet*, *King Lear*, *Romeo and Juliet*, and *Macbeth*; and histories, including *Richard II*, *Richard III*, and *Henry V*.

Mix It Up

Prior to Shakespeare, most English drama used rhyming verse. Shakespeare and other dramatists of his time began writing plays using both verse and prose, often mixed throughout the play depending on the character or the scene. Shakespeare typically used blank verse, which doesn't rhyme but does have an iambic pentameter rhythm.

THE LEGACY

Shakespeare died on April 23, 1616. For over 400 years, people around the world have read and performed his works, both in the original English and in at least seventy-five other languages. The plays continue to be staged for sold-out audiences in theaters and are also reinterpreted time and time again in books and movies. His influence has permeated our very language—the first use of more than 1,500 words can be traced back to his poems and plays—and he coined many common phrases we use daily.

JOHN DONNE (1572–1631)

The Paradoxical Poet

John Donne is not an easy poet to characterize, for many reasons. Born a Roman Catholic during the Renaissance, he later converted and became a priest in the Anglican Church. Although now a well-known poet, during his lifetime he published very few poems and was better known for his sermons. He is counted as a leading member of the Metaphysical poets, a designation that did not exist in his lifetime and was originally used as an insult. His poems can be erotically charged and sexually explicit, but also extol the virtues of a long and happy relationship or marriage. His reputation has risen and fallen and risen and fallen over the years, as poetic and cultural tastes have changed. His poetry itself can be difficult to parse, filled with paradoxes and unexpected twists of logic.

A DIFFICULT LIFE PATH

In 1572, John Donne was born in London into a Catholic family during the reign of the Protestant Queen Elizabeth. His father, John, was an ironmonger who died when Donne was four years old. Donne's mother, Elizabeth Heywood, a grandniece of the martyred Sir Thomas More, remarried soon after. As a teen, Donne attended both Cambridge and Oxford universities, but earned degrees from neither because they both required an oath to the Anglican Church for graduation. He went on to study law in London. In 1593, Donne's younger brother died of the plague while in prison for the crime of harboring a Catholic priest. The arrest and death must have shaken Donne; a year later he joined the Anglican Church.

In his mid-twenties, Donne served as private secretary to Sir Thomas Egerton, Lord Keeper of the Great Seal of England. Donne became a member of Parliament in 1601. That same year, he secretly married Sir Egerton's sixteen-year-old niece, Anne More, an act unpopular with her relatives. He was fired and briefly thrown in prison, and Anne's dowry was withheld. He and Anne were rich in love but poor in wealth and struggled financially for most of their sixteen-year marriage. They raised a large family: Anne gave birth to twelve children. She died in 1617, shortly after their twelfth child was stillborn.

Did You Know?

Playwright Margaret Edson's play, *Wit*, features the poetry of John Donne extensively in its script. *Wit*, which won a Pulitzer Prize for Drama in 1999, is told from the perspective of Vivian Bearing, an English literature professor and Donne scholar who is dying of ovarian cancer. Vivian grapples with her own mortality through the lens of Donne's poems.

Given his strident Catholic upbringing and youth, it's surprising how large a role the Anglican Church played in Donne's life as an adult. He was ordained as an Anglican priest in 1615 and worked for the Church in a variety of capacities, including serving as royal chaplain. In 1621, he became Dean of St. Paul's Cathedral. He was a gifted preacher and many of his sermons and reflections on Christianity were collected and published both in his lifetime and after.

POETRY OF CONTRASTS

Donne was prolific during the 1590s. Most of the poems eventually compiled into his two major volumes of work, *Satires* and *Songs and Sonnets,* were probably written during this period. Although these collections were not officially published until around 1633, after Donne's death, a circle of friends and fellow poets circulated and read his poems during his lifetime.

Donne wrote in a variety of poetic forms, including satire, elegies, lyrics, epigrams, songs, and sonnets. He returned again and again to several themes, especially love, religion, and death. Although he wrote poems exclusively on some of these subjects, he often mixed and matched his themes in complex ways, such as finding and articulating divinity in both sex and love and writing poems that grappled with spirituality and its relationship to death.

Donne was an expert at using the literary device of conceit, where two things are compared in an unlikely and surprising but imaginative way. For example, one of his most famous poems, "A Valediction: Forbidding Mourning," uses an extended conceit to compare two lovers to the legs of a drafting compass. His poetry is also often filled with paradoxes, or contradictions, that exist not only between poems in his canon but also within the text of individual poems. He is rarely mild in his emotions. We find love poems that are ecstatic and love poems where the poet is writing in despair. Donne drew from art, theology, and philosophy when writing, but he did so with wit and humor.

Metaphysical Poets

The term *Metaphysical poets* applies loosely to a group of seventeenth-century English poets, including Donne, Richard

Crashaw, Henry Vaughan, George Herbert, Andrew Marvell, and Abraham Cowley. It's a misleading characterization: the Metaphysical poets didn't necessarily write about metaphysics. The poets John Dryden and Samuel Johnson derisively characterized their style of writing as metaphysical for being unnatural and too concerned with showing off their learning. The Metaphysical poets approached spiritual and philosophical topics with reason, logic, and intellect. Like Donne, many used the literary device of conceit in their poems. Largely ignored during the eighteenth and nineteenth centuries, they came back into fashion during the twentieth century. Modernist poet T.S. Eliot was instrumental in reviving interest in their style of poetry in the 1920s.

"'Tis true, 'tis day; what though it be?
O wilt thou therefore rise from me?
Why should we rise, because 'tis light?
Did we lie down, because 'twas night?
Love, which in spite of darkness brought us hither,
Should in despite of light keep us together."

—"Break of Day," John Donne

RELIGIOUS POETRY

Reformation and Reverence

Religion and poetry are close bedfellows. The artfulness of verse lends itself exceptionally well to expressing matters of faith and religion. In this book, we began our discussion of poetry by examining the work of Greeks and Romans, who beautifully rendered the tales of their gods and goddesses into verse. They were not the only ancients who found verse a suitable way of expressing faith. Almost all cultures and religions have a poetic tradition of their own. The Hebrew Bible, or Old Testament, for one, is a text rich with poetic language. King David sang and recited poetry and is said to be the author of many of the verses found within the Psalms.

Whether they are inspired to respond to a sacred text—in Western culture, generations of poets have found inspiration within the pages of the Bible—or are contemplating their own personal moral and spiritual path, religion is a common subject for many poets. Some of the greatest poems ever written can be characterized as religious poetry.

THE SIXTEENTH AND SEVENTEENTH CENTURIES

Reformers introduced English-translated versions of the Bible into England, first by John Wycliffe in the late fourteenth century, and later by William Tyndale in the sixteenth century, but they were considered heretical by the state and the Catholic Church. Tyndale was burned at the stake in 1536. When Henry VIII parted ways with the Roman Catholic Church, things changed rapidly. In 1539, Henry VIII authorized the first English Bible, allowing its use in Church of England services.

Paradise Lost

Although the Cambridge-educated poet John Milton (1608–1674) wrote poems early in his career, he was widely known in his lifetime for his prose publications advocating for the anti-Royalists during England's Civil War. His legacy, however, rests firmly with *Paradise Lost*, an epic poem written during the 1650s and first published in 1667. Milton's concerns with religious and political liberty are reflected in the poem, which tells the story of creation and Adam and Eve's temptation and fall from grace in the Garden of Eden. It is one of the most widely regarded and studied texts from its era. In 1671, Milton published *Paradise Regained*, essentially a sequel, which is a brief epic about the temptation of Christ in the wilderness.

The political and religious upheaval of the Renaissance period, as England transitioned from a Catholic nation to a Protestant one, was reflected in the poetry of its time. As discussed in the section about John Donne, the Metaphysical poets often approached spiritual topics. Donne's *Holy Sonnets*, a collection of nineteen religious poems published after his death, profoundly portrays his very personal struggles with the divine, which included converting from the Catholic to the Anglican Church. His contemporary, George Herbert, who lived from 1593 to 1633, composed devotional poems, which were collected and published in 1633 as *The Temple: Sacred Poems and Private Ejaculations*. Educated at Cambridge, Herbert served as the university's orator before becoming an Anglican priest in 1630. *Temple* was incredibly popular for its day, reprinted twenty times in the forty years after it was published. The poems portray Herbert's deep faith and are praised for their natural meter, direct style, and language.

The Puritan poet Anne Bradstreet (1612–1672) wrote lyrically about her personal religious convictions. In 1630, she emigrated to New England with her husband, Simon Bradstreet, and her parents. Her poetry is pious but also honest about her struggles with the concepts of sin and salvation. Bradstreet was America's first published poet: her first collection of poems, *The Tenth Muse*, was printed in London in 1650.

EIGHTEENTH AND NINETEENTH CENTURIES

As the Age of Enlightenment dawned in the eighteenth century, with its emphasis on philosophy and science, religious poetry became less culturally prominent. As the century waxed on, fewer and fewer poems were published on religious themes. The Romantic poets, many of whom were born in the late 1700s, would begin exploring spiritual themes again, albeit generally with a lot of skepticism. They ranged in temperament from Percy Bysshe Shelley, an atheist; and William Blake, a fundamentalist Christian; to Samuel Taylor Coleridge, a Unitarian. Blake's poetry is the most overtly religious, although it breaks frequently from the strict teachings of the Church of England. The Romantics placed an emphasis on the self, preferring to pursue spiritual satisfaction at an individual, not institutional, level. Naturally, their poetry reflects those values.

THE VICTORIANS

Religious beliefs shifted again during the Victorian era. Scientific advances, including Darwin's discoveries, caused many long-held beliefs to be questioned. Although the Church of England remained the official state church, Protestant movements such as Methodism had taken hold and encouraged the lower classes to practice their faith through a personal experience of the Holy Spirit. Religious themes of temptation, sin, and redemption are found frequently in the work of Victorian poets. Christina Rossetti wrote highly devotional poetry. Matthew Arnold, on the other hand, struggled with a loss of faith in his poetry, most famously in his short lyric "Dover Beach."

Gerard Manley Hopkins was a Victorian Jesuit priest whose poetry is infused with his Christian faith and his belief that "The world is charged with the grandeur of God." In fact, all of his poems are religious and are considered on a par with the work of Donne and Herbert. Although he was a Victorian, his poetry is often characterized as Modern, since his style is more characteristic of the 1920s and 1930s, when it was published, than with his own contemporaries.

MODERN ERA

Characterizing religious poetry in the Modern era can be difficult. Although religion and faith still play a role in modern life, they are not subjects generally viewed with the same intensity in Western culture as they were in earlier eras. Major poetic movements of the twentieth and twenty-first centuries have not been characterized by their treatment of or attitudes toward religious subjects, as earlier eras have been.

Religion is certainly not absent from Modern poetry, though. The carnage of the World Wars in the 1900s caused many poets to turn to questions of faith. The civil rights and the antiwar movements of the 1960s also influenced a number of poets who used religious concepts and morality to interpret current events. The advent of technology has caused poets to examine the place humans have in the universe. In the last few decades, as the world has become increasingly global thanks to both technology and immigration, we've seen an increase in English-language poems by people of faiths other than Christianity, by poets practicing Native American, Hindu, Buddhist, Jewish, and Islamic belief systems.

ART AND POETRY

Art Shedding Light on Art

From classic times until today, poets have drawn—pardon the pun—inspiration from the art world. The ancient Greeks coined the term we use today for poems focused on works of art: *ekphrasis*. Ekphrastic poetry, in ancient Greece, meant poetry that closely and vividly described art.

Some of the earliest examples of ekphrastic poetry are found in Homer. In a passage from *The Iliad*, Homer described in detail, for almost 150 lines, Achilles' shield:

"First fashioned he a shield, great and sturdy, adorning it cunningly in every part, and round about it set a bright rim, threefold and glittering, and therefrom made fast a silver baldric. Five were the layers of the shield itself; and on it he wrought many curious devices with cunning skill."
—*The Iliad*, Book 18, Line 478, Homer (Augustus Taber Murray translation)

Homer's continued description of the shield is teeming with life. He populated the shield with images of brides at weddings, musicians playing flutes, young men dancing, and farmers plowing. His descriptions are so detailed that a reader—or listener—of the poem can almost "see" the shield as perfectly as if in real life. Homer set the bar for ekphrastic poetry incredibly high, but that hasn't stopped later poets from attempting to achieve similar results with their own descriptions.

EKPHRASTIC POEMS

In the centuries since, poets have played with the idea, expanding the definition to include more than just descriptions of art. Ekphrastic poems are poems in which the poet engages in verse with a piece of art or an artist, and can include an effort to find a larger meaning or symbolism in the artwork. The subject of ekphrastic poetry can be any form of art, whether paintings, sculptures, or photography.

One of the most celebrated ekphrastic poems is "Ode on a Grecian Urn," by Romantic poet John Keats, published in 1819. Keats had visited the British Museum and viewed the Greek artifacts on display, although the specific urn described in this poem is probably a figment of Keats's imagination. The poem is brief, at least compared to Homer. In five ten-line stanzas written in iambic pentameter, the poet, like Homer, contemplates scenes of life in ancient Greece. Keats, rather than simply describe the scenes chiseled on the urn, chose to have his narrator address the urn directly, asking questions of it that can never be answered: "What men or gods are these? What maidens loth?"

The tone is melancholy as he considers all the unfinished actions on the urn: the leaves that cannot ever fall off the marble tree; the lovers whose lips will never touch in the intended kiss; the empty village streets that will never be populated. He takes a close examination of an object and turns it into a profound musing on life and eternity, noting the urn will remain long after the deaths of those who have viewed it. He concludes, cryptically, since it's hard to know if the "Ye" is humanity or the urn, by writing:

> "'Beauty is truth, truth beauty,—that is all
> Ye know on earth, and all ye need to know.'"
>
> —"Ode on a Grecian Urn," John Keats

Another well-known set of examples is based on Pieter Brueghel's painting *Landscape with the Fall of Icarus*. In the painting, a man plows a field along the edge of a sea. Not far below him, unnoticed by the farmer, Icarus's legs are seen in the sea, probably moments before he is completely submerged. Two famous poets have written about the painting: W.H. Auden published "Musée des Beaux Arts" in 1940 and William Carlos Williams published "Landscape with the Fall of Icarus" in 1962. Auden's poem is more complex, while Williams, in his characteristic style, is sparse, but the interpretations of both poets can help viewers of the original painting see it in a new light.

In 1899, *The San Francisco Examiner* published a poem by Edwin Markham, "The Man with the Hoe." The poem is based on the painting of the same name by Jean-François Millet, which shows an exhausted man leaning on his hoe. In Markham's poem, the hard-working man becomes a symbol of the oppression faced by laborers. The poem took on a life of its own, reprinted in newspapers across the country, and helped spark a national conversation on fair working practices for agricultural laborers.

Ekphrastic poems have never really gone out of style. The Victorians—who loved to travel and write about their travels—were fans of using them to describe the art they encountered while abroad. For some Modern poets, the artistic process forms the poem's subject. Mark Doty's 1953 poem "To Jackson Pollock" makes the leap from the poet viewing a snapped ginkgo tree to the act of Pollock painting one of his vast canvases. It can also include the experience of visiting a museum, as in Derrick Austin's 2015 poem "Taking My Father and Brother to the Frick," which uses the museum visit and his relatives' bored reaction to the art within as a foil for revealing his relationship with them.

In the following eighteenth-century poem, poet Phillis Wheatley praises artwork by her fellow slave and friend Scipio Moorhead. Wheatley compares her efforts as a poet to his as a painter, pointing to the peace and immortality their work will bring them.

> "To show the lab'ring bosom's deep intent,
> And thought in living characters to paint,
> When first thy pencil did those beauties give,
> And breathing figures learnt from thee to live,
> How did those prospects give my soul delight,
> A new creation rushing on my sight?"

—"To S.M., a Young African Painter, on Seeing His Works," Phillis Wheatley

Further Study

For more examples of poetry inspired by art, see the following list. Many of these poems, and the art that inspired them, can be viewed online:

- "My Last Duchess" by Robert Browning
- "The Shield of Achilles" by W.H. Auden
- "Nine Nectarines and Other Porcelain" by Marianne Moore
- "The Starry Night" by Anne Sexton
- "Hopper: *Confessions*" by Anne Carson
- "Stealing *The Scream*" by Monica Youn

NEOCLASSICAL POETS

Reasonable and Refined

The Neoclassical period is roughly from 1660 until 1798. The poetry and literature of the day is characterized by a love of reason. Neoclassical writers also placed a lot of value on philosophy, refinement, and a healthy dose of skepticism. They prized wit and intellect over feeling and imagination. As the name might imply—the new classicists—they were fans of the Greek and Roman classical cultures.

The period is divided into three subperiods:

1. The Restoration (1660–1700)
2. The Augustan Age (1700–1745)
3. The Age of Sensibility (1745–1798)

Let's take a closer look at each Neoclassical subperiod and at the poets who flourished in them.

The English Civil War

During the 1640s, England, Scotland, Ireland, and Wales were devastated by a bloody Civil War, when Royalists fought Parliamentarians for control of the government. In 1649, King Charles I was executed. In 1651, his son, Charles II, fled England. For the next nine years, England was under Puritan rule, first by Parliament and then by Oliver Cromwell, who had been one of the military leaders for the Parliamentarians during the Civil War. After Cromwell died, his son was named to replace him but lasted less than a year in power. Subsequently, Charles II was recalled to England and crowned in 1660, restoring England's monarchy.

THE RESTORATION (1660–1700)

Charles II took the throne on May 29, 1660. After more than ten years of turmoil, England was calm again. Writers, like everyone else, were weary of all the political and religious fights. Neoclassicism had already taken hold in France, and English writers followed suit with their own works.

John Dryden (1631–1700): Dryden was a prolific poet, critic, translator, and playwright who is considered one of the greatest writers of the seventeenth century. He was poet laureate of England from 1668-1688. As a poet, he is best known for his satirical work, including *Absalom and Achitophel*, a political satire against the Earl of Shaftesbury; *Mac Flecknoe*, a scathing lampoon of fellow poet Thomas Shadwell; and *The Medall*, which sharply ridiculed Shadwell again, as well as Whig leaders. Like Chaucer, Dryden wrote almost flawlessly in heroic couplet, rhyming iambic pentameter. He also translated works by Homer, Ovid, and Boccaccio for inclusion in a narrative poetry collection, *Fables Ancient and Modern*.

THE AUGUSTAN AGE (1700–1745)

Writers during this era were inspired by, and often imitated, the writers Virgil, Horace, and Ovid from the original Augustan Age (63 B.C.E.-C.E. 14). Augustan writers valued order and logic in their writing, none more so than Alexander Pope, the poet most closely associated with this era.

Alexander Pope (1688–1744): Pope began writing poems from a young age, imitating the masters of earlier eras, and went on to create numerous highly regarded poems of his own. Writing in strict heroic couplet, his pastoral poetry—poems that glorify rural life—were among his best. They include the collection *Pastorals* and the poem *Windsor-Forest*, which described the land and history surrounding his home with an optimism typical of Augustan poets. He was a witty satirist, who gleefully skewered in verse the celebrities of the day. *The Rape of the Lock*, a satire written in the style of Homer's *The Iliad*, brilliantly and beautifully mocks a real-life schism between two noble families when a gentleman cut off a lock of a young woman's hair. In *The Dunciad*, written semi-anonymously as Scriblerus, he mocks his literary enemies with thinly disguised caricatures. He also translated the original *Iliad* into English pentameter couplets, a task he financed by soliciting individual subscriptions. Pope's death in 1744 drew the Augustan Age to a close.

The Graveyard Poets

The graveyard poets were a group of eighteenth-century writers obsessed with death and grieving who wrote meditative, morbid poetry. Poet Thomas Gray (1716–1771) was a prominent member whose poem "Elegy Written in a Country Churchyard" is considered a masterpiece of the genre. Although they weren't Romantics, their work is considered a precursor to that later literary movement.

Lady Mary Wortley Montagu (1689–1762): A talented writer best known for her witty letters, especially those known as the "Turkish Embassy Letters," Montagu was also a poet. She taught herself Latin and Greek and translated poems from classical sources over the course of her life. She wrote in many poetic forms, including epics, lyrics, and ballads. As a satirist, one of her best-known works is "Verses Address'd to the Imitator of the First Satire of the Second Book of Horace," a scathing retort to her once-friend Alexander Pope, who portrays her unflatteringly as Sappho in his *Moral Essay II*.

THE AGE OF SENSIBILITY (1745–1798)

The Age of Sensibility is also sometimes called the Age of Johnson, after Samuel Johnson, who was the most prominent writer of the era. The Age of Sensibility is characterized by a softening of the rules followed by poets earlier in the Neoclassical period, paving the way for the Romantic period. Poets in this period began moving away from larger philosophical concerns in their writing, choosing instead to express individual feelings.

Samuel Johnson (1709–1784): Johnson, a poet, essayist, and critic, is also the author of *A Dictionary of the English Language*. Johnson's poem *The Vanity of Human Wishes* is an imitation of Juvenal's "Tenth Satire" in which Johnson writes earnestly and passionately in heroic couplet about the vanity of ambition.

Thomas Gray (1716–1771): Gray is responsible for the lines "where ignorance is bliss / 'Tis folly to be wise." An eloquent poet, he composed both serious sonnets and odes as well as humorous mock-heroic poetry, including "Ode on the Death of a Favourite Cat Drowned in a Tub of Goldfishes." Critics bemoan, however, that most of his poetry fails to rise to the brilliance displayed in his "Elegy Written in a Country Churchyard."

William Cowper (1731–1800), Thomas Percy (1729–1811), and William Collins (1721–1759): These three are responsible for some of the best poetry produced by Sensibility poets. Cowper helped bring blank verse back into fashion; Percy revitalized interest in ancient English poetry and ballads, edited for modern tastes; and Collins was a master at creating musical pentameter couplet, as demonstrated in his *Persian Eclogues*.

BALLADS

Sing Me a Story

Ballads possess a rich and ancient heritage, stemming back to the stories people told one another while huddled around the kitchen fire or gathered for a wedding or feast. While epics may recount a hero's lengthy adventures, a ballad is more succinct. It can be told, or better yet, sung in a matter of a few minutes. Ballads are a European folk tradition and were probably spread by traveling minstrels during the Middle Ages.

WHAT IS A BALLAD?

The definition of a ballad is not all that precise. It's essentially a story poem told with short stanzas.

Ballad Characteristics
- The words *ballad* and *ballet* are both derived from the Latin verb for dance: *ballare*. Ballads may have begun as accompaniments to folk dancing.
- Ballads are narrative poems. They are stories with plots.
- Ballads can be written on a variety of topics, including love, religion, politics, and death.
- Repetition is common in ballads. A refrain may be repeated after every other stanza. Or, the wording with each repetition may change slightly to give the meaning a twist.
- Ballad style isn't rigid, but a popular format features four-line stanzas with alternating lines rhyming. It is also common to have the alternating lines have four and three beats for the rhythm.

Ballade with an "E"

But wait—there's more. There's also a ballade—with an "e." That's a little different, although related. Ballades were sung by French court poets in the fourteenth century. Chaucer was the first to try it in English: his poems "To Rosemounde" and "Balade de Bon Conseil" were written as ballades. A few other poets in the fifteenth century imitated Chaucer but the style fell out of favor until the nineteenth century. Ballades are brief, only three stanzas connected by a refrain and shared rhymes.

COLLECTING AND CATALOGUING

The earliest English example of a ballad is found in the British Library. "Judas" is included in the Harley Manuscript, a collection of early English poems of many styles compiled around 1340. We know ballads were popular in the Elizabethan era, when they were written down and sold cheaply as broadsides. Broadsides were large folio sheets printed on one side only.

In later centuries, collecting and publishing folk ballads became popular. The eighteenth-century Scottish poet Robert Burns helped to compile more than 300 traditional Scottish ballads for two multivolume collections, *The Scots Musical Museum* and *A Select Collection of Original Scottish Airs for the Voice*. Fellow Scot Sir Walter Scott, the nineteenth-century poet and novelist, was also a keen ballad collector. His compilation *Minstrelsy of the Scottish Border* included both traditional ballads and Scott's own imitations.

The largest and most thorough collection of ballads was compiled and published by folklorist F.J. Child. *The English and Scottish Popular Ballads* was the product of extensive research by Child.

Commonly referred to as the Child Ballads, the collection was published in ten volumes from 1882 to 1898. The volumes contain 305 songs, listed alongside alternative versions, including American ones, with copious notes. The folk music scene of the 1950s and 1960s drew heavily from the Child Ballads for inspiration.

FAMOUS BALLADS

"Lord Randall": Sir Scott included this anonymous folk ballad in his 1802 ballad collection. It is an Anglo-Scottish border ballad that relates the conversation between a son and his mother when he returns home after being poisoned by his lover. The poem consists of ten repetitive, four-line stanzas, which reveal simply and efficiently the basic plot lines of a dramatic story arc. Throughout the poem, three phrases are repeated to finish each of the first three lines of each stanza; the entire fourth line is repeated every time.

"Oh where ha'e ye been, Lord Randall my son?
O where ha'e ye been, my handsome young man?"
"I ha'e been to the wild wood: mother, make my bed soon,
For I'm weary wi' hunting, and fain wald lie down."

"Where gat ye your dinner, Lord Randall my son?
Where gat ye your dinner, my handsome young man?"
"I dined wi' my true love; mother, make my bed soon,
For I'm weary wi' hunting, and fain wald lie down."

—"Lord Randall," Anonymous

The Rime of the Ancient Mariner: The Romantic poets of the nineteenth century were particularly keen on ballads, and some of the best examples of the form were written by them. Samuel Taylor Coleridge's *The Rime of the Ancient Mariner* was first published in 1798 in *Lyrical Ballads*, a ballad collection coauthored with William Wordsworth. The ballad tells the story of a mariner who kills an albatross while on a sailing trip near Antarctica. His action brings a curse down on him and his crew. Coleridge's language mimics the traditional ballads of earlier centuries and tells a rather convoluted tale with themes of guilt, sin, and redemption.

"The Ballad of Nat Turner": Poet Robert Hayden included "The Ballad of Nat Turner" in his poetry collection *A Ballad of Remembrance*, published in 1962. Hayden used a traditional form of four-line stanzas for his seventeen-stanza ballad, but he opted for inconsistency in his rhyming structure. The poem uses repetition sparingly. Nat Turner was an American slave who led a bloody rebellion in 1831. Turner hid for six weeks after the insurrection, before his capture and execution by hanging. Hayden's poem does not tell the story of the rebellion. Instead, his focus is quieter and dreamlike, told from the perspective of Turner as he wanders, prays, and has visions during his escape.

ROBERT BURNS (1759–1796)

The Bard of Scotland

Robert Burns is a treasured and beloved figure in Scotland and beyond. More than 200 years after his death, he still serves as an ambassador of Scottish culture and language to people all around the world. He wrote his poetry in the Scots language, a distinctive dialect with its own grammar and vocabulary, about traditional Scottish life and traditions. His poetry helped foster a sense of pride in Scotland for his eighteenth-century Scottish readers and, to this day, is still a rallying cry for Scots nationalism.

THE POET-FARMER

Robert Burns was born in Alloway, Scotland, on January 25, 1759, to William and Agnes Burnes. (They later changed the spelling.) He grew up in poverty, the eldest of seven children. Burns's father was a gardener who later become a tenant farmer. Burns grew up working long hours in the fields to help his father. He received a few years of formal education but was largely tutored at home or self-taught. By his own admission, corroborated by the observations of others, he was bookish. His studying proved fruitful: references to the work of other eighteenth-century poets, as well as to the Bible and Shakespeare, are abundantly evident in his poetry.

When Burns was twenty-five, his father died bankrupt, after his farms had failed to produce a profit for several years. Burns continued to farm, but he also used the period after his father's death to enjoy drink, song, and female companionship. Despite his bookish reputation, Burns was also rather a ladies' man. In 1785, Elizabeth Paton gave birth to his first child; in 1786, Jean Armour birthed his twins. Neither young lady was his wife at the time of the births. During this period, Burns was busy writing poetry, and sharing the poems locally, both as manuscripts and as performances.

Burns raised money for his first poetry book by soliciting subscriptions. In 1786, 612 copies of *Poems, Chiefly in the Scottish Dialect* were printed in Kilmarnock. A copy or two made it to Edinburgh, where Scotland's cultural elite resided, and were well received. Burns saw the opportunity and headed to Edinburgh. His rural upbringing and polished poetry provided a contrast appreciated in the city, where there was growing interest in Scotland's cultural heritage. A year later, a new edition of his book was published to widespread acclaim. Burns used his payment to take two trips, one to the Scottish border towns and the other through the East Highlands.

Burns Suppers

Every year on or near January 25, Burns fans gather in homes and halls to celebrate his birthday, a practice that began not long after his death. His poetry is read, haggis is served, whisky is drunk, and speeches are made, all following roughly the same script, no matter where in the world the dinner takes place. They can be a lot of fun for attendees, even for people who don't normally read a lot of poetry.

By 1788, he had married Jean. Over the next eight years, Burns's national reputation as a gifted poet would grow and solidify. He dedicated himself to preserving Scotland's traditional songs, collecting, editing, and writing poems for the tunes in superb imitation of traditional styles. He and Jean moved to Ellisland, where he became an excise officer and returned to farming, but their financial situation was dire. Burns had suffered throughout his life from heart disease, probably caused by malnourishment and overwork as a child, and the return to farming proved fatal. Burns had fathered at least twelve children, legitimate and illegitimate. He died at the age of thirty-seven on July 21, 1796. Jean gave birth to his last child, Maxwell, shortly after his death.

POETRY AND NATIONALISM

Burns was writing during the historical period associated with the Neoclassical poets and just prior to the emergence of the Romantics. His work in many ways stands apart. He was the product of a long, insular, literary tradition in Scotland, and by some critical assessments, he represents the end of that tradition. In the nineteenth century and since, England's influence over Scotland has changed the national character, including its literature.

Burns created more than his share of memorable poems. We have him to thank for the line "O my luve's like a red, red rose." He also gave us the words to "Auld Lang Syne," which has gained worldwide fame as a song played at midnight on New Year's Eve, and "My Heart's in the Highlands." His poems cover the subject of love extensively, often extolling the virtues and beauty of a fair lass in one poem and his winsome wife in another. He wrote passionately and joyfully about Scotland's history, landscape, and people. *The Cotter's Saturday Night* is a particularly moving portrayal of Scottish farm life, told warmly and without condensation. He was also gifted at comic satire. In *Tam O'Shanter*, he uses the heroic pentameter couplet to retell a Scottish legend of a drunken farmer who stumbles on a witches' party in the ruins of a church.

Burns was a firm believer in the equality of all man, an attitude that did not gain him friends among the wealthy who had praised and feted him when his poems were first published. His poem "A Man's a Man for A' That" expresses this belief in heartfelt form by comparing the poor to the wealthy and showing their shared humanity. It culminates in the stirring lines "That Man to Man, the world o'er, Shall brothers be for a' that."

What Is *Scots*?

The Scots language is not simply English spoken with a Scottish accent. Scots refers primarily to Scottish dialects spoken in the Lowlands. Although similar to English, it is characterized by a distinctive vocabulary and grammar. In Scotland today, Scots is one of three native languages still in common use, along with English and Scottish Gaelic, an ancient Celtic language. Under English rule, speaking and writing in Scots was discouraged, but the language survived and continues to hold a valuable place in Scotland's cultural and artistic heritage.

ROMANTIC MOVEMENT (1789–1824)

Let's Get Emotional

The Romantic movement lasted, at most, forty-five years, by the most generous of interpretations, but it was a period of intense literary activity. Romanticism produced some of the most well-known and beloved English poets of all time, including William Wordsworth, Samuel Taylor Coleridge, William Blake, Lord Byron, John Keats, and Percy Bysshe Shelley. Many of them were good friends and collaborators. (We will discuss the latter three at length in subsequent sections.) It was an era when poets were on the front lines of the day's political and social upheavals, and their poetry helped shape the nation's psyche. They differed in style and temperament but shared a revolutionary spirit and a strong belief in the need for an equitable society. Their poetry rejected the Neoclassical ideals of reason and logic. Instead, they embraced feelings and the power of imagination.

What's My Name?

Lord Byron certainly knew the word *romantic*, but he wouldn't have used it to describe his poetry. The Romantic poetic movement in England didn't get called that until the middle of the nineteenth century. Applying the term *Romanticism* made it simpler for critics and readers to discuss their collective work.

WHY ROMANTICISM?

Romantic poetry grew out of a tumultuous time in history. Parliament ruled England instead of a king, but the country had yet to become a true democracy. America had gained its independence, after a difficult, draining war that lasted from 1775 until 1783. Then, the French Revolution began in 1789 and sent shock waves through Europe, as France's ancient aristocracy was bloodily ousted from power. In the aftermath, a wave of democratic ideas rolled through Europe and forcefully swept into England. Politics became radicalized.

"Bliss was it in that dawn to be alive
But to be young was very heaven!"

—"The French Revolution as It Appeared to Enthusiasts at Its Commencement," William Wordsworth

---

Other changes were afoot too. By the late eighteenth century, England was in the throes of an Industrial Revolution. Starting around 1760, technological advances meant a shift from handmade goods to those produced by machines. Factories sprang up throughout the country, but especially in the previously rural north of England. Agriculture practices had changed, and many people who had previously earned a living farming were getting pushed off their ancestral lands.

Looking for work, people flooded the cities that formed around the mills and factories. The period from 1760 until 1850 marks the biggest social change in Britain's history: the transfer of huge portions of the population from the countryside to cities. The south of England was no longer the most populated area of the country, and London was no longer the nation's only major metropolis. Cities brought a middle class that demanded a more equitable political system. They also fostered poverty on a scale not seen in England since the Middle Ages. Without the support of their village communities, many people operated without a safety net.

Lyrical Ballads

Wordsworth and Coleridge published *Lyrical Ballads* jointly in 1798 under neither's name. Widely considered to be the launch of the Romantic movement, most of the poems were by Wordsworth, including the highly regarded blank verse "Tintern Abbey," but there were also several notable ones by Coleridge, including *The Rime of the Ancient Mariner*. The second edition included a famous "Preface" by Wordsworth, arguing that poetic language should reflect real language and poems should take "humble and rustic life" as their subject.

This was the era in which the Romantics came of age. In their poetic style and in their subject matter, we see a reflection of the intense changes happening in the world around them. Let's look at some of the basic qualities and traits that distinguish their work from both their Neoclassical predecessors and their Victorian successors.

Key Themes and Characteristics of Romanticism
- **Self-expression and individualism:** Romantics wrote poems expressing their own personal experiences.
- **Nature:** They viewed nature both as a source of enjoyment and as an almost mystical substitute for religion.

- **Dreamlike and highly imaginative poems:** The Romantics weren't afraid to take a flight of fancy.
- **Concern for the poor:** They used poetry to draw attention to the less fortunate.
- **The wisdom of youth:** "The Child is father of the Man," as Wordsworth wrote in his poem "My Heart Leaps Up."
- **God-complex:** They viewed themselves as visionaries, called to help change society.

WILLIAM WORDSWORTH
(1770–1850)

As a young man, Wordsworth visited revolutionary France twice. When he returned to England in 1792, he left behind his pregnant French girlfriend. Although his family had intended he pursue a career in the Anglican Church after studying at Cambridge, Wordsworth was more interested in pantheism than in Christianity. He moved to the Lake District, where he collaborated with Coleridge on the *Lyrical Ballads* and, in 1802, married Mary Hutchinson. (Later, the label Lake Poets was applied to Wordsworth, Coleridge, and Robert Southey.) He created a large body of work over the course of his lifetime and was highly influential to other poets, especially in his use of a natural style. He was named England's poet laureate in 1843. His pantheistic and revolutionary ideals softened with age, angering some of the later Romantic poets, but his work overall was instrumental in elevating the "common man." He died in 1850, leaving Mary to publish his seminal work *The Prelude*, an autobiographical, blank-verse poem. Published in fourteen volumes, it turned the concept of an epic poem inside out, tracing the poet's philosophical adventures rather than the poet-hero's physical feats and challenges.

SAMUEL TAYLOR COLERIDGE (1772–1834)

A poet and critic, Coleridge was not as prolific as some of his peers, but his work is considered vitally important to the Romantic movement. Coleridge had Unitarian leanings as a young man and collaborated with Robert Southey to envision a pantisocracy, an equal-government-for-all commune in America, which was never acted on. An opium addict throughout his life, Coleridge's symbolic poem, the ode "Kubla Khan," may have been the by-product of a drug-induced dream. The poem is written with rich imagery and showcases the Romantics' embrace of the imagination. His narrative poem *Christabel* draws heavily from the style and form of folk ballads. He is also known for pioneering a style of conversation poems, written in blank verse. He used this intimate tone, which was imitated and refined by subsequent generations of poets, in "This Lime-Tree Bower My Prison" and "Frost at Midnight," among others.

WILLIAM BLAKE (1757–1827)

Blake is an iconic figure in English poetry and art, although his poetry was not widely appreciated until after his death. Even now, many view it as challenging to interpret. A devout Christian but highly critical of the established church, much of his poetry grapples with ideas of personal spirituality and with his own sense of mysticism. (He saw visions as a child and adult and occasionally prophesied.) His political views were in line with his theological ones, emphasizing the individual and self-autonomy, and he was critical of oppressive regimes. He wrote several poems in response to the American and French Revolutions. The poetry found within one of his most famous works, *Songs of Innocence and of Experience*, provides a powerful statement of social protest. Like Wordsworth, Blake wasn't afraid to write about issues such as poverty and child exploitation in his poetry. Blake was also a talented artist and much of his reputation also rests on his paintings and engravings. A trained printer, Blake developed a style of book he called illuminated printing, engraving copper plates with detailed illustrations surrounding each poem. He used the method for *Songs of Innocence and Experience*, and went on to use his artwork to illustrate and enhance the written meaning of many other self-published editions of his poems.

JOHN KEATS (1795–1821)

A Talented Youth

John Keats was a standout member of the second generation of Romantic poets, a distinction even more remarkable when you consider his life was cut short at the tender age of twenty-five. During his brief life, Keats produced some of the most memorable poems in English literary history, including "Ode on a Grecian Urn." He was a poet who subscribed to the philosophy of aestheticism, believing that art exists purely for the sake of beauty.

A LIFE CUT SHORT

Keats, unlike some of the other Romantic poets, did not come from a privileged background. He was born in London on October 31, 1795, the eldest son of Frances and Thomas Keats, a livery-stable keeper. By the time he was eight and entered John Clarke's school in Enfield, he had two younger brothers and a sister. Classmates described him as well liked, not particularly scholarly, and an occasional fighter. That same year, 1804, his father died in a riding accident. His mother quickly remarried but then separated from her new husband. During the upheaval, Keats and his three younger siblings moved in with his widowed maternal grandmother. By early 1810, his mother had returned, but she died of tuberculosis later that year, when Keats was fourteen.

By that point, Keats had become a more active student and read and wrote voraciously under the tutelage of his headmaster, whose son was Keats's good friend. During those brief years, Keats crammed, learning French, translating Greek mythology, and reading histories. This happy situation was not to last. His grandmother had received a generous inheritance from her late husband, and appointed two trustees, Richard Abbey and John Rowland Sandell, to act as guardians for her grandchildren. Abbey took over and mismanaged the funds, creating financial strain for Keats and his siblings throughout their lives.

Perhaps because of that strain, Keats left school at fourteen to begin an apprenticeship with a local surgeon/apothecary. While doing the apprenticeship, he stayed in contact with his headmaster's family, walking miles to their home to continue his literary studies. Through them, he read *The Faerie Queene* by sixteenth-century English poet Edmund Spenser. The poem lit a fire in Keats, introducing him to allegorical romance. From that point on, around the age of eighteen, Keats was smitten by poetry. He began to study poets and to write some poetry of his own, while continuing his medical internship. He earned his apothecary license and did further study and work at Guy's Hospital in London in 1815, but his heart was not in it.

Keats found a mentor in poet Leigh Hunt (1784–1859), who was affiliated socially and professionally with both Percy Bysshe Shelley and Lord Byron, with whom he coedited a journal called *The Liberal*. Hunt introduced Keats to Shelley, and their ensuing friendship helped Keats develop as a poet.

The Sweetness and the Sorrow

The year 1818 was a significant year in Keats's life. His brother Tom contracted tuberculosis, and Keats nursed him for his last months, until his death in December. Around the same time, Keats fell in love with Fanny Brawne. His grief over his brother and his joy at experiencing love for the first time had a profound, maturing effect on his subsequent poetry.

Although they were engaged at one point, Keats and Fanny never married. In February 1820, Keats began coughing up blood and knew immediately he was dying of tuberculosis. Attempting to stave off his death sentence, he traveled to Italy with a friend, the painter Joseph Severn, in September. The Italian climate wasn't enough to save him. He died in February 1821 in Rome. He requested his own epitaph for his grave: "Here lies one whose name was writ in water."

A ROMANTIC AT HEART

Keats's relationship with Leigh Hunt moved him into a new phase in his development as a poet. As a protégé to Hunt, Keats initially imitated Hunt's poetic style, which relied heavily on rhymes. Keats did not, however, gravitate toward Hunt's political activism. Hunt and his brother ended up in prison for two years after publishing an attack on the prince regent.

Keats—against the advice of Shelley—published his first volume of poetry, *Poems*, in 1817. The next year, he published *Endymion*, a long romance based on Greek myth. Critics were not impressed, derisively calling his work part of the "Cockney" school of poetry. Class and political conflict are partly to blame for the poor reviews— Hunt's leftist politics rubbed off on Keats—but the poetry itself was weak and uneven in quality compared to his later work. Even in these less-than-perfect poems, though, Keats had begun exploring the themes that would define him, the pursuit of beauty tempered by a clear-eyed and startlingly honest view of reality. Keats's poetry found its tension, and greatness, in the exploration of contrasts and opposites.

Beauty Wins

The criticism was devastating but Keats used it to his advantage, working harder at his craft. Despite—but probably a result of—his intensive life experiences in 1818, Keats entered into an intensely productive period of writing in September 1818. By September 1819, he had produced most of the work that his reputation now rests on. He began work on the unfinished epic *Hyperion*, written in blank verse after Milton. He wrote the pseudo-medieval narrative poem *The Eve of St. Agnes*, using rich, detailed imagery and evocative rhymes that give the poem a musical quality. The lyrical poem *Lamia*, written in pentameter couplets, uses a Greek myth about a female demon to pit the concepts of beauty and imagination against philosophy. In Keats's version, beauty is clearly the preferred winner.

During this period, Keats also mastered the poetic style of ode, a lyric poem that takes the form of an address, usually praising the object spoken to. Three of his greatest odes are "Ode to a Nightingale," "Ode on a Grecian Urn," and "Ode on Melancholy." His final book of poetry, *Lamia, Isabella, The Eve of St. Agnes, and Other Poems*, was published in 1820.

"Ah! dearest love, sweet home of all my fears
And hopes and joys and panting miseries,—
To-night, if I may guess, thy beauty wears
A smile of such delight,
As brilliant and as bright,
As when with ravished, aching, vassal eyes,
Lost in a soft amaze,
I gaze, I gaze!"

—"To Fanny," John Keats

Keats's poetry was on a trajectory for even greater heights had he lived. He published fifty-four poems in his lifetime, but it took later generations to fully recognize his brilliance. His tragic, early death left a gaping hole in the legacy of the Romantics.

PERCY BYSSHE SHELLEY (1792–1822)

The Romantic Atheist

Percy Bysshe Shelley packed a significant amount of life and writing into his twenty-nine years. Shelley was married twice, lived in England and Europe, was close friends with many other prominent writers of the day, and wrote some of the century's most beautiful lyric poems. He courted controversy, openly touting his atheism, his social justice ideals, and his freewheeling ideas on love. His attitudes gained him both admirers and detractors. Regardless, his work holds up as some of the finest produced during the Romantic era.

AN UNUSUAL GENTLEMAN

Shelley was born in 1792 into a wealthy, aristocratic family. He was the eldest child of Timothy and Elizabeth Shelley and was heir to his grandfather's large estate and peerage. He grew up with one younger brother and four younger sisters. Like others of his class, he was educated at boarding schools, beginning at age ten at Syon House Academy, followed by Eton. As a sensitive and imaginative boy who was an atheist from a young age, Shelley experienced more than his share of teasing and bullying at both institutions. While at Eton, he began writing poetry and was influenced by his reading of *The Monk*, a Gothic novel by Matthew "Monk" Lewis. Shelley's first publication was a Gothic novel, *Zastrozzi*. In it, the villain Zastrozzi articulates many of Shelley's own heretical and atheistic viewpoints.

In 1810, he went up to study at Oxford. While there, he met Thomas Jefferson Hogg, a fellow student who became a dear friend. They shared a common interest in science, philosophy, magic, and religion, and collaborated on poetry. Their decision to write, publish, and circulate a pamphlet titled *The Necessity of Atheism* resulted in their expulsion, less than a year after Shelley had arrived at the university. Shelley probably could have been reinstated had he apologized and declared himself a Christian, but he refused. As a result, he became estranged from his father, who cut him off from the family's fortunes until he came of age two years later.

Free Love

In August 1811, nineteen-year-old Shelley eloped with sixteen-year-old Harriet Westbrook. They spent much of their brief marriage in England and Wales, where Shelley distributed his radical political pamphlets. They had a daughter, Elizabeth Ianthe, in June 1813, and a son, Charles, in November 1814, but by that point the marriage had fallen apart. Shelley had formed a friendship with the philosopher William Godwin, whose radical views on personal freedom, anarchy, and atheism were appealing to the young poet. Godwin's daughter with his late wife, the feminist Mary Wollstonecraft, became involved with Shelley. The younger Mary Wollstonecraft essentially eloped with the still-married Shelley in 1814. Mary was seventeen when she and Shelley traveled together to Europe for six months, accompanied by her stepsister, Claire Clairmont. A proponent of free love, Shelley extended an invitation to Harriet to join them. She declined.

Shelley's grandfather died in January 1815, easing Shelley's financial burdens. Mary and Shelley bounced back and forth between Europe and England for a while, spending time in Switzerland with their good friend, the poet Lord Byron. Over the course of their relationship, Mary and Shelley had three children who all died very young. The first daughter (b. February 1815) died shortly after birth; their son William (b. January 1816) died of malaria at age three; and their daughter Clara (b. 1817) died as a toddler. Their fourth child, Percy Florence (b. November 1819), was the only one to reach adulthood. The Shelleys formed a literary power couple: Mary was also a talented writer who published the novel *Frankenstein* in 1818, and went on to publish several more over her lifetime.

In December 1816, Harriet committed suicide, drowning herself in the Serpentine, a lake in Hyde Park, London. Shelley was deemed unfit to raise their two children, who were placed in foster care. He soon married Mary. They lived in England for a while before moving permanently to Italy in early 1818. During the next four years he produced his major works. His life ended much too early. At age twenty-nine, in 1822, he drowned in a storm in Italy while on a sailing excursion.

POETRY OF THE SUBLIME

Although he published poetry as a youth, *Queen Mab: A Philosophical Poem* was his first important work. *Queen Mab* was a political epic, published in 1813, and used poetry to convey the same political viewpoints as his pamphlets: a desire for freedom from oppressive regimes, whether political, social, or religious. Shelley had been privately writing poems since his marriage to Harriet. When his volume of poems *Alastor: or the Spirit of Solitude and Other Poems* was published in 1816, it was clear he was maturing as a poet. The style is similar to Wordsworth and skillfully uses symbols and mythical sources. Much of Shelley's poetry shows the influence of the older poets Wordsworth and Coleridge, but he approaches topics such as nature and religion with more skepticism.

In the following years, Shelley's poetry would cover political topics, including advocating for a bloodless revolution, as well as highly personal poems in response to his children's deaths and angst over his growing estrangement from Mary. In 1820, he published *Prometheus Unbound*, a lyrical drama in four acts, which some consider his masterpiece. Infused with idealism, the play uses Greek mythology to create a political allegory in which revolution leads to an era of love.

Much of his work shows Shelley's struggle with authority. While in Italy, he wrote political poems targeting specific government officials in England. These were deemed even by his friends to be too dangerous to publish. Shelley was more versatile than he is often given credit for—in his repertoire there are also satires; lighter, humorous poems; and conversation poems in the style of Coleridge. After his death, Mary compiled much of his work and had it published, but some would not see the light of day until the twentieth century. As much as he was a product of his day, Shelley was also far ahead of his time.

"Adonais": A Funeral Elegy

Percy Bysshe Shelley honored his friend and rival John Keats with "Adonais," a funeral elegy. The beautifully written pastoral elegy was published in 1821. Although the poem promotes the mistaken believe that Keats died of a broken heart because of poor reviews, it is widely considered to be a touching tribute to Keats's poetic legacy and is one of Shelley's best poems.

LORD BYRON (1788–1824)

The Bad Boy Romantic

George Gordon, Lord Byron, is one of the most well known of the Romantic poets. He is famous almost as much for his eccentric life as he is for his poetry. Despite the fuss made over his unusual lifestyle, he truly was a gifted poet whose works are still viewed as important literary accomplishments.

ECCENTRIC YOUTH

Born in 1788 to an aristocratic family, Byron's childhood was not a happy one. His father, John "Mad Jack" Byron, and his Scottish mother, Catherine Gordon of Gight, were unhappily married. His father spent most of his mother's wealth, prompting her to leave him shortly before she gave birth to Byron. Born with a clubfoot, he was forced to undergo painful medical treatments as a child. He was abused, sexually and physically, by his nurse. When he was ten, he inherited his title as the sixth Baron Byron and the family moved into Newstead Abbey, a grand but dilapidated mansion.

His mother raised him sternly as a Calvinist, giving him a solid foundation in biblical studies, but he rejected her religion in favor of atheism. At Cambridge he established a reputation as an eccentric, keeping a pet bear in his student rooms at Trinity College, and generally living it up as a partier. In 1809, he embarked on a two-year Mediterranean adventure. He did not leave his eccentricities behind—he dressed in Albanian costume for part of the trip and, at one point, decided to recreate the Greek legend of Leander's swim across the Hellespont to see his love, the goddess Hero. He returned to England in 1811 and, by 1812, found success and fame as a poet.

For the next four years, Byron publicly caroused as a playboy in English society and engaged in dalliances with a number of women, and probably men. Rumors even flew that he had an incestuous relationship with his half sister, Augusta Leigh. He briefly settled down in 1815 as the husband of the prim Anne Isabella Milbanke, but they were ill-matched. The marriage failed not long after she gave birth to their daughter. Despite the public antics, Byron showed a more serious side in his role as a politician in the House of Lords, advocating passionately for social reforms.

A Revolutionary Mathematician

Lord Byron's daughter Ada Lovelace (1815–1852) is called the world's first computer programmer. Her mother, Anne Isabella Milbanke, ensured Ada was tutored extensively in mathematics. Lovelace was later mentored by mathematician Charles Babbage, who conceived of a project called an analytical engine, which was essentially a computer. Lovelace translated a paper about the engine, adding in her own notes with calculations and a program for the machine, as well as prescient insights into the potential uses for computers.

Departure from England

In 1816, Byron left England permanently. While living in Switzerland, he enjoyed a close friendship with fellow Romantic poet Percy Bysshe Shelley and traveled with him and Mary Wollstonecraft Godwin. While there, he had an affair with Mary's stepsister, Claire Clairmont. Claire subsequently gave birth to their daughter, Allegra, who died very young. He traveled on to Italy, where he found many more sexual partners, including a nineteen-year-old Italian noble-woman, Teresa Guiccioli, who happened to have an elderly husband.

In 1822, Shelley was drowned. Byron, grieving the loss of their six-year friendship, distracted himself by heading to Greece. He became involved, financially and personally, in Greece's war for independence with Turkey. While in Greece, he contracted malaria and died a week later, on April 19, 1824. His body was returned to England for burial.

The Byronic Hero

Many of Byron's poems feature protagonists with similar characteristics. A Byronic hero is a dashing young man who undertakes dangerous adventures. He has a mysterious past, a guilty demeanor, and is much adored by the women he encounters. Byron disavowed autobiographical aspects of his hero's lives, but the public loved conflating the poet with his fictional avatars.

"WE'LL GO NO MORE A ROVING"

It took time for Byron to find his voice as a poet. As a teen, he wrote a collection of poems, many highly erotic, published anonymously as *Fugitive Pieces*. He burned almost all of the copies. At nineteen, his second effort, a collection of lyric poems titled *Hours of Idleness*, was not well received. In 1809, he published *English Bards and Scotch Reviewers*, a heroic couplet poem written in the satirical style of Alexander Pope. Pope had gone out of style by that time, although *English Bards* was critically praised more than his earlier efforts.

Byron's trip to Europe helped him find maturity as a poet. He used the trip as inspiration to write a travelogue featuring a young man named Harold, the first Byronic hero. Harold's quest for self-fulfillment resonated with readers. Byron published the first two cantos of *Childe Harold's Pilgrimage* in 1812 to immediate success—the first printing sold out in three days. He had to adjust to almost instant fame. He published the remaining cantos in 1818, but first he followed up the success with additional verse stories, written in a hurry in either tetrameter or heroic couplets. These included *The Giaour*, *The Bride of Abydos*, and *The Corsair*. Each poem starred its own egotistical hero, whom readers swooned over, providing a rakish prototype for later novelists and writers to imitate.

As a poet, Byron functioned both as a Romantic and a realist. Some of his works are quite dark and gloomy, but they were written in proximity to his airier poems. His ability to shift gears is a testament to his skills as a writer. Reflecting his status as a true Romantic, emotions run high in his poetry.

Over the course of his career, Byron skillfully experimented with different meters. During the seven years he lived in Italy, he wrote some of his best work using ottava rima, a ten-syllable version of an Italian stanza style. The original consisted of eight eleven-syllable lines with a rhyme scheme of *abababcc*. Byron used it for several satirical epic poems, including *Beppo*, a satire of Venetian manners, published in 1818, and *The Vision of Judgment*, which skewers fellow English Romantic poet Robert Southey. He displayed his creativity fully in his last epic poem, *Don Juan*, still somewhat a work-in-progress when he died in 1824. Considered a masterpiece on a par with Pope's *The Rape of the Lock*, the poem's wide-ranging narrative shows Byron at his best.

"So, we'll go no more a roving
So late into the night,
Though the heart be still as loving,
And the moon be still as bright.

For the sword outwears its sheath,
And the soul wears out the breast,
And the heart must pause to breathe,
And love itself have rest.

Though the night was made for loving,
And the day returns too soon,
Yet we'll go no more a roving
By the light of the moon."

—"So, We'll Go No More a Roving," Lord Byron

LOVE POETRY

Roses Are Red, Violets Are Blue

Who doesn't love a good love poem? The expression of love is why poetry was invented in the first place, right?

That may or may not be true, but there is no question that love is one of the most common themes addressed in poetry. Poets adore wrangling with love on the page, almost as much as they do with death and nature. Some write chastely, adoring their beloved from afar. Others capture a naughtier vibe, celebrating love in a physical sense. We tend to think of love poems as romantic, but some explore the love a parent has for a child, and vice versa, or recognize the special bond between friends. Where the heart goes, so to, poetry goes.

COURTLY LOVE

If you've ever read and enjoyed a love sonnet, you have the fourteenth-century Italian poet Petrarch to thank. He didn't invent the form, but he made it so popular that poets for centuries afterward were scrambling to mimic his style. The concepts of courtly love were introduced by troubadours in the courts of twelfth-century Europe, exemplified by the court of Eleanor of Aquitaine. Petrarch drew on these concepts, as well as the sonnet form which had developed by at least the thirteenth century, when composing his poetry.

Petrarch's brand of love falls into the unattainable category. He claims to have seen "Laura" at a church service on April 6, 1327. He probably never saw her again, if she even existed, but that didn't stop him from composing 366 poems about her, including 317 sonnets.

The collected poems are called either the *Rime Sparse* or the *Canzoniere*. His heart bleeds fourteen lines at a time for his unrequited—never reciprocated—love.

Petrarchan Sonnet Characteristics

- A male poet addresses a lady.
- The lady must be unattainable.
- All of her characteristics will be idealized.
- He will praise her physical beauty in great detail. (This is called *blason*.)
- There are usually many metaphors.
- The poet remains humble and miserable in love.

Famous Lines of Love

"To be loved, be lovable." —Ovid

"One half of me is yours, the other half yours." —William Shakespeare

"If ever two were one then surely we." —Anne Bradstreet

"O my Luve's like a red, red rose." —Robert Burns

"And oh! that eye was in itself a Soul!" —Lord Byron

"How do I love thee? Let me count the ways." —Elizabeth Barrett Browning

In the sixteenth century, English poets adopted the form. Sir Thomas Wyatt translated Petrarch's sonnets, but also composed ones of his own. The English courts of Henry VIII and Queen Elizabeth were a welcoming place for poets. Although idealized love still held a fascination for writers of that era, they shifted the conventions. Sometimes, as in many of Shakespeare's love sonnets, a male is addressed. Love also gets expressed more in physical, not just platonic, terms. Love is obtainable: Edmund Spenser in *Amoretti* composed sonnets for his future wife. Love poems became a coded way to share political or religious concerns, as well.

POEMS TO LOVE ABOUT LOVE

Where to start? Hearts swell and hearts break with each new generation of poets. We could fill an entire library with nothing but love poems, and books would still be overflowing out the door. Let's take a deep breath, step back, and choose a few—just a few—poems to consider as representatives of verses on love.

"Sonnet 18" by William Shakespeare

Opening with the classic line, "Shall I compare thee to a summer's day?" this sonnet contains some of the most beautiful lyrics found in English poetry. Scholars now believe Shakespeare wrote the sonnet for a young man but it applies to love between any gender. Over the course of the poem, Shakespeare changes his mind about the summer metaphor for his love, determining that while "summer's lease hath all too short a date" his love's "eternal summer shall not fade."

"The Sun Rising" by John Donne

In this seventeenth-century aubade (a poem for early morning), Donne chastises the sun for shining on him and his lover while they are in bed. Filled with romantic swagger, he brags that he can block the sun's rays with just a wink, but he won't because he doesn't want to stop gazing on his bedmate. Donne's infatuation with his lady is so encompassing that he finishes the poem by telling the sun it shines on the entire world when it shines on them. In just thirty lines, Donne perfectly captures the self-contained universe experienced by two people who have fallen in love.

"Bright Star" by John Keats

A love sonnet written, most likely, to Keats's fiancée Fanny Brawne. (It may be the last poem he ever wrote, after he knew he was dying of tuberculosis.) Like Shakespeare, Keats is fixated on the idea of eternity. He addresses a star, envying its fixed vantage point in the sky, where it watches the moving waters of the oceans and snow falling on mountains. In line nine, he rejects the star's solitariness. Instead, he wants to be steadfast and unchangeable while resting on his "fair love's ripening breast." He'll stay there forever, "or else swoon to death."

"She Walks in Beauty" by Lord Byron

This classic poem, written in three six-line stanzas, expresses the poet's appreciation of a young lady's beauty. Technically, he never says he's in love with her, but it seems likely, given how he gushes about her appearance, as well as her mind and heart. Byron uses simile to great effect in this poem, drawing a comparison between the beauty of one woman and that of all nature: "She walks in beauty like the night / of cloudless climes and starry skies."

"To My Valentine" by Ogden Nash

Not all love poetry has to be super serious. Ogden Nash's delightful twentieth-century poem "To My Valentine" uses twenty lines to express the nearly twenty ways he loves his Valentine. The poem, however, turns the usual love poem on its head and is not filled with beautiful imagery. Instead, Ogden uses comparisons to hate and loathing to demonstrate the intensity of his own love. He manages to work in allusions to the Axis powers, a hangnail, a stinging wasp, and a shipwrecked sailor. The result holds a mirror up to hatred, showing the passion of love.

"Another Valentine" by Wendy Cope

Cope's poem is short and sweet and celebrates long-term love. It was commissioned by the British newspaper *The Daily Telegraph* in 2009. In it, Cope addresses her partner, expressing an obligation to be romantic because it's Valentine's Day. Their relationship is a well-established love, and the poet almost seems ready to scoff at the idea of romance after so long. And yet, by discussing romance, the poet begins to feel it and offers love to her valentine.

WHAT MAKES A GOOD LOVE POEM?

Inspired to write your own love poem? What can a modern poet possibly say that hasn't already been said before? Scottish poet Carol Ann Duffy, Britain's 2009 poet laureate, tackled the problem head on in her 2005 poem aptly named "The Love Poem." Duffy cleverly composed the poem using lines from famous love poems, including lines from Shakespeare, Donne, Barrett Browning, Walter Scott, and the Bible. The result is surprisingly poignant.

Some tips for creating an original poem: Write honestly. Be specific. Use concrete images. Tell a story. Imagine the poem as a conversation. Write in a comfortable style—you don't have to force your thoughts into rhymes. Write multiple drafts.

THE VICTORIANS

A Period of Rapid Change

Not every queen gets her own literary era named after her, but then, not every queen is Queen Victoria. In 1837, she took the throne of the United Kingdom of Great Britain and Ireland and ruled an astounding sixty-three years. Her time was one of great industrial and scientific advances, political and social changes, and religious upheaval. Both in England, and across the pond in the United States, writers flourished. Poets now competed with novelists for the public's attention. While some writers continued to look to the past for inspiration, others felt compelled to experiment, pushing the definition of poetry into new and exciting territory.

Great English poets of the era include Elizabeth Barrett Browning; Emily Brontë; Christina Rossetti; Alfred, Lord Tennyson; Matthew Arnold; Robert Browning; Oscar Wilde; and Gerard Manley Hopkins.

HISTORY LESSON

Queen Victoria's reign covered the better part of a century. It's helpful to break it down into three periods.

1. **1837–1851: Early Victorian Period.** A period of unrest and hunger for many of Britain's citizens, as the country transitioned from an agricultural to an industrial economy. The railways were built, transforming how goods and people could move throughout the country.

2. **1851–1870: Mid-Victorian Period.** Wealth, power, and influence returned to Britain. Beginning in the late 1850s, it began to rapidly expand its colonial possessions in Africa, India, the Middle East, and Asia. The Church of England had lost its monolithic grip, splintering into factions ranging from evangelicals to High-Church traditionalists. A large proportion of Brits simply stopped attending church. Charles Darwin published his theory of evolution in 1859 in his seminal work *On the Origin of Species*.

3. **1870–1901: Late Victorian Period.** This period was marred by war with colonial territories and competition economically with both Britain and the United States. Trade unions developed during this period, and the very end of the century found women organizing in increasing numbers to demand voting rights. Photography and sound recording flourished, making it easier for future generations to look back at and study the Victorians.

VICTORIAN POETS

What defines Victorian poetry as *Victorian*? No one poetic form dominated the era. Poets wrote sonnets, lyrics, ballads, narratives, and, quite popularly, limericks. When reading Victorian-era poems, keep in mind the rapid changes that happened in society during their time. Nostalgia was important to some poets. For source material in his narrative poems Alfred, Lord Tennyson looked back to medieval Arthurian legends. Elizabeth Barrett Browning saw poetry as a means for social change, a way to push attitudes forward on rights for women, children, the poor, and the oppressed. Some found solace in their faith. Christina Rossetti wrote ballads rich with symbolism. Gerard Manley Hopkins experimented with rhythm and language in his devout poetry, so aggressively he wasn't published until 1918, nearly thirty years after his death. Matthew Arnold used his poems to express his religious doubts. Sex appears, too, covertly, in many Victorian poems.

The following poets are among the most well known from this era. We'll examine a few more in greater detail in coming sections.

EMILY BRONTË (1818–1848)

Although Brontë is mainly known as the writer of the novel *Wuthering Heights*, she was also a talented poet. In 1846, she self-published, with her sisters Charlotte and Anne, under a pseudonym, a collection called *Poems by Currer, Ellis, and Acton Bell*. The slim volume contained twenty-one of her poems and sold only two copies. Well after her death, 200 of her poems would be collected and published. Her poetry was written in a spare, clean manner—critics have called her style earthy—grounding her concepts with concrete images. She wrote about faith and a longing for freedom but rejected many of the conventions of organized religion.

> "Fall, leaves, fall; die, flowers, away;
> Lengthen night and shorten day;
> Every leaf speaks bliss to me,
> Fluttering from the autumn tree.
> I shall smile when wreaths of snow
> Blossom where the rose should grow;
> I shall sing when night's decay
> Ushers in a drearier day."
>
> —"Fall, Leaves, Fall," Emily Brontë

ROBERT BROWNING (1812–1889)

Browning and his wife, Elizabeth Barrett Browning, formed the equivalent of a Victorian poetry power couple when they wed in 1846. Both were established poets at the time and had initially formed a friendship based on their shared interest. Browning is now a giant figure when we think of the Victorians, but his reputation took time to develop. He didn't achieve fame until he'd been writing for twenty years. His greatest legacy is the use of dramatic monologues in his poems, including "My Last Duchess," in which a Duke stands before a painting of his late wife, regaling a courtier with increasingly chilling observations about her. In the process, he essentially confesses to her murder. Browning's approach of making characters think out loud in a conversational style was unusual for his time. It was a technique that heavily influenced twentieth-century poets, including Ezra Pound and T.S. Eliot.

CHRISTINA ROSSETTI (1830–1894)

Rossetti's father was an Italian political refugee; one of her brothers was the poet and painter Dante Gabriel Rossetti. In her time, Rossetti was often considered a poet for children. Later critics have looked at her work through the filter of feminism. Rossetti wrote using simple diction and a sing-song rhythm that belied the deeper themes and complexity in her work. (One of her volumes of poetry is even titled *Sing-Song*.) Her most famous poem is *Goblin Market*, a ballad that never settles into a predictable meter. The idiosyncratic result contributes to the mystical aspects of the fairy-tale poem, in which two sisters are preyed upon by evil goblins. Rossetti was a Christian whose work often reflected her morality. In *Goblin Market,* she tells a morality tale with common Christian themes of temptation and redemption.

The Rhymers' Club

Oscar Wilde and William Butler Yeats were two of the members in this poetry group, which met in London in the 1890s, sometimes gathering in private homes but often in an upstairs room of Ye Olde Cheshire Cheese pub in Fleet Street. All male, the poets would exchange work and offer one another critiques. The group published two volumes of poetry during the 1890s, which were reprinted again in the 1970s. Yeats credited the group with helping him learn his trade as a poet.

ELIZABETH BARRETT BROWNING (1806–1861)

An Innovative Victorian

Elizabeth Barrett Browning was a precocious talent who published her first collection of poems as a fourteen-year-old. In an era when women were still treated like second-class citizens, Barrett Browning stands out as unusually independent, outspoken, and opinionated. Her story is not one of obscurity: her prodigious talent was recognized and lauded in her own time. She was the more famous poet in her marriage to Robert Browning, a love affair launched by a shared passion for poetry.

A PRECOCIOUS GIRL

Elizabeth Barrett Browning was born near Durham, England, in 1806 to Edward and Mary Barrett Moulton. Barrett Browning's family had for generations owned plantations in Jamaica. One of twelve children, she was raised in Herefordshire, England, on a 500-acre family estate, Hope End. Her upbringing did not include formal schooling, but she was well taught at home and was encouraged in her desire to read. By around the time she was ten, she was reading Shakespeare and history books and had taught herself Greek and Latin so she could read the Roman and Greek classics. An interest in the Old Testament prompted her to take on Hebrew, as well.

At fourteen, she self-published a four-book epic poem in the Greek style, called *The Battle of Marathon*. Her next publication, the anonymous *An Essay on Mind, with Other Poems*, was equally ambitious, especially given the young age of its author. Published in 1826, the volume traced the development of philosophy, science, history, and poetry from the classical era to the present. The poems revealed a keen intelligence but not an accomplished poet.

Barrett suffered from ill health in her youth. Her spine was injured in an accident while saddling her pony, and she also contracted a lung illness, which was treated with morphine. Her family's wealth began to dissipate when the Jamaican plantations faltered due to mismanagement and abolition movements. Shortly after her mother's death when Barrett was in her early twenties, the family was forced to move from their estate into rental cottages in Sidmouth, on the coast. Barrett Browning continued to write, publishing *Prometheus Bound*, a translation of Aeschylus, in 1833.

Success As a Poet

When she was thirty, Barrett Browning moved to London with her overbearing father. Her first well-reviewed collection, *The Seraphim, and Other Poems*, was published in 1838. *Seraphim* was praised in England and the United States as the work of a promising young poet. The title poem, a lengthy dialogue conveying the theological conversation of two angels observing Christ's crucifixion, was harder for critics to love but the shorter poems in the collection were widely praised.

Barrett Browning's personal life became fraught for the next few years. Her father sent her to live on the coast in Torquay, hoping to improve her ill health. While there, her favorite brother, Edward, was drowned. Distraught, Barrett Browning became a recluse. She returned to London and spent five years sequestered in her home, supported by an inheritance and cared for by her family, but seeing few others. She used the time to write, publishing in journals, and gradually accumulated enough poems to warrant a new publication. *Poems*, published in 1844, was a critical and popular success.

Almost Poet Laureate

When William Wordsworth died in 1850, leaving the role of Britain's poet laureate open, Elizabeth Barrett Browning was seriously considered. Instead, the title went to Alfred, Lord Tennyson. Although she wasn't selected, it is a testament to her reputation that she almost made it. In 1668, John Dryden was the first to hold the title of poet laureate for England. In 2009, Carol Ann Duffy was the first woman to be given the title.

Poems also proved instrumental in changing Barrett Browning's personal life. The poet Robert Browning loved *Poems* and wrote the author in January 1845 to tell her so. Their letters—574 of them—blossomed into love, and after meeting, they made plans to marry. Barrett Browning's father was vehemently opposed to her marrying anyone, so the couple was forced to secretly marry on September 12, 1846.

They soon moved to Italy. Whether it was the weather or the restorative effects of being in love, Barrett Browning's health greatly improved. She gave birth to Robert on March 9, 1849, in Florence when she was forty-three years old. Barrett Browning remained a prolific writer for the rest of her life and produced some of her best and most celebrated work after her marriage. She died in 1861 after a brief illness.

COMMON THEMES EXPLORED BY BARRETT BROWNING

Here are some of the topics covered in Barrett Browning's poems.

Love

Barrett Browning was six years older than her husband and, due to her ill health, had never expected to marry. She secretly composed forty-four love sonnets before and after her wedding. The poems reveal her trepidation about their relationship, her wonder at their growing love, her gratefulness for his admiration and, eventually, her acceptance and return of that love. At Browning's urging, she published them as "Sonnets from the Portuguese" in a revised edition of *Poems* in 1850. The title was meant to disguise their true meaning. "Portuguese" is taken from a nickname that Browning had for his wife (he said that her skin tone was dark, making her look as if she was of Portuguese origins), and the title gives the impression that they are translated poems. The poems are now widely considered some of the best love poetry ever written. Part of their appeal is their perspective: it was exceedingly rare to read sonnets written by a woman.

Social Justice

Barrett Browning tackled some of the most contentious social and political issues of the day in her poetry. In "The Cry of the Children," published in *Poems* in 1844, she decried the deplorable conditions for children working in factories and mines, not only vividly describing their lives but condemning all of Britain for turning a blind eye to their suffering. The 1850 version of *Poems* included "The Runaway Slave at Pilgrim's Point," written from the perspective of a female slave who is raped and ultimately murders her "too white" infant son. The poem sharply addresses not only the evils of slavery, but also the religious institutions that sanctioned it. She courted controversy after moving to Italy, writing passionately about Italian politics, championing Italian independence, in *Casa Guidi Windows* in 1851 and *Poems Before Congress* in 1860.

Feminism

The roles and rights of women were frequently debated by Victorians, who lumped all such discussions of equality under the phrase "The Woman Question." Barrett Browning contributed to those discussions through her poetry. She used female protagonists in several of her ballads to grimly illustrate the inequalities in power, love, and sex experienced by Victorian women. In 1856, she approached "The Woman Question" by publishing a long narrative, sometimes called a novel-poem, titled *Aurora Leigh*. Loosely autobiographical, the work tells the story of Aurora Leigh, a fiercely independent poet who navigates significant gender and social barriers to build a successful writing career for herself. Despite its radical subject matter, the poem was incredibly popular and was published in multiple editions over the next several decades.

ALFRED, LORD TENNYSON (1809–1892)

Alfred, Lord Tennyson is one of the most recognized poets of the Victorian period. Although his popularity has waxed and waned in the years since he first published classic poems such as "The Lady of Shalott," no one can question the profound artistic influence he wielded during his lifetime. Not only was he granted a peerage in 1883 based on his poetic talent but he held the role of Britain's poet laureate for an unprecedented—and still unmatched—forty-two years.

CHILDHOOD AND YOUTH

Tennyson's childhood was anything but ideal. He was born on August 6, 1809, in Somersby, Lincolnshire, as the fourth of twelve children to Elizabeth and George Tennyson, a rector in the Anglican Church. George was an alcoholic who sometimes turned violent. Although George Tennyson was the eldest son in a wealthy family, his father favored his younger brother as his heir, creating intense tension in the extended family. Mental illness was an ever-present reality for Tennyson's relatives. Tennyson's mother and father both suffered from depression, one of his brothers was confined to an insane asylum, and another was a violent alcoholic. Most of his siblings, at some point in their lives, required treatment for a mental breakdown. Epilepsy also ran in the family. Tennyson occasionally experienced trances throughout the first half of his life and lived in constant fear that his symptoms would evolve into epilepsy.

Most of Tennyson's education happened at home, where his father gave him a good background in Greek and Latin and provided him free rein to read through his library. Tennyson was a quiet, introverted child who was drawn to poetry. When he was seventeen, he published his first collection, *Poems by Two Brothers*, which nominally included a few poems by his brothers Charles and Frederick. The book was not a success.

A DEVELOPING POET

In 1827, he followed his two older brothers up to Trinity College at the University of Cambridge. At Cambridge, Tennyson found his tribe. He fell in with a group of other young poets and intellectuals, and spent at least some time as a member of The Apostles, an exclusive, scholarly student group. Among these friends was Arthur Hallam, the son of a famous historian and incredibly smart in his own right, who forged a close friendship with Tennyson. Hallam, and others, encouraged Tennyson in his writing. While still a student, in 1830 he published *Poems, Chiefly Lyrical*. Tennyson became Tennyson with that collection, which included "The Kraken" and "Mariana." His impressive talent with language and ability to write beautifully on a level achieved by few poets, let alone one so young, was on clear display. It took time for reviews to appear, but when they did, most praised the young poet's efforts.

By this point, Tennyson had introduced Hallam to his family, including his younger sister, Emilia, who went by Emily. That summer, Hallam and Tennyson made the first of two trips to Europe together. They headed to Spain, in theory to assist Spanish rebels in their revolutionary war, but that focus of the trip never really materialized. Regardless, Tennyson would use the trip—and the Spanish landscape—as inspiration in poems for years to come.

In 1831, George Tennyson died suddenly, leaving his family in debt. There was no more money for Cambridge, and Tennyson and his brothers were sent home without degrees. In 1832, he published *Poems*, which included "The Lady of Shalott," "The Hesperides," and "The Lotos-Eaters." The reviews were vicious, and Tennyson took nine years to lick his wounds, refusing to publish, although he continued to write. That summer, he and Hallam, who by that point was officially engaged to Emily, traveled together to Germany.

A year later, in 1833, twenty-two-year-old Hallam died suddenly, probably of an aneurism, while traveling abroad with his father. His death devastated Tennyson, who suffered a severe depression for years.

A Giant Grows

Tennyson scraped by for the next ten years, essentially couch surfing among his friends and relatives, and living off a small allowance. In 1842, he published again, a two-volume collection, *Poems*. Success was sudden. He'd finally cracked the code for popular and critical adoration. He'd revised many of his earlier poems and included new ones, written in a variety of styles. His next publication was a long narrative poem, *The Princess*, similar in theme to Elizabeth Barrett Browning's *Aurora Leigh*. In Tennyson's poem, the independent young woman at the center of the plot is a medieval princess who champions women's rights. Critics hated it but the Victorian populace ate it up.

In 1850, he published *In Memoriam A.H.H.*, a series of elegies for Hallam, a work widely considered to be his masterpiece. (We'll discuss it more in this book's "Death and Poetry" section.) The poem solidified Tennyson's position as one of the greatest poets of his era and he was named William Wordsworth's successor as poet laureate. That same year, he married Emily Sellwood, with whom he'd had an on-again, off-again relationship for more than fifteen years. They had two sons, Hallam and Lionel.

A Comfort to Queen Victoria

When Queen Victoria's husband, Prince Albert, died in 1861, she was wracked with grief. She donned black widow garb and remained officially in mourning for the rest of her life, even though she lived another forty years. She turned for solace to Tennyson's poetry, and was quoted saying that, "Next to the Bible, *In Memoriam* is my comfort."

A Beloved Figure

The grief Tennyson experienced after his friend Hallam's death profoundly affected much of his writing. In addition to *In Memoriam*, reflections of his grief are seen in other poems, including "Ulysses" and "Morte d'Arthur." The latter was part of a cycle of poems, *Idylls of the King*, about Arthurian legends, which glorified heroic values. He was a proud Englishman, and his love of country is evident in his *Ode on the Death of the Duke of Wellington*, a public work commissioned when he was the poet laureate. It is also reflected in "The Charge of the Light Brigade," written in response to a contemporary battle in the Crimea in which six hundred British cavalrymen were ordered by tragic mistake to charge into, as Tennyson writes, "the valley of Death." The ballad honors the fallen soldiers and captures the pulse of battle with short lines written in dactylic dimeter.

Although he wrote several narrative poems, he didn't excel at characterizations and dialogue. Later efforts at writing plays fell painfully flat, despite his great talent. Lyrics, where he was free to express his own thoughts and feelings, were his sweet spot. Tennyson possessed the ability to write with soaring language and natural cadence and rhythms. His facility with language sometimes prompted critics to accuse him of being all beauty and not enough substance, brutally arguing he wasn't intellectual enough. Tennyson's poetry, however, addressed many of the biggest issues of the day—including women's equality, the role of morality in a culture where the church was losing authority while science gained it, mental health, and the Industrial Revolution.

Tennyson continued to write until the end of his long life. He was a beloved poetic figure and celebrity, known for his big voice and stylish clothing. His books continued to be bestsellers even long after his death. He passed away on October 6, 1892, and joined Chaucer in the Poets' Corner of Westminster Abbey.

DEATH AND POETRY

The Eternal Sleep

Like love, death is a universal human experience, so it's not surprising that death is one of the most common subjects for poetry. While some poets write about grief after the loss of a loved one from a very personal perspective, other poets have approached the subject as a means of exploring larger universal themes, including the meaning of life. The topic is large enough to hold philosophical, emotional, and intellectual explorations. In the hands of the best poets, a poem about death can provide solace and comfort, not to mention a feeling of shared humanity.

ELEGIES

There are fine examples of poems about death in nearly every style of poetry, but the most common form is an *elegy*. The term has its roots in the Greek word *elegeia*, meaning "lament." Greeks and Romans considered any poem using an elegiac couplet—a dactylic hexameter followed by a dactylic pentameter—to be an elegy, whether the subject was death, love, or war. (An elegiac couplet is also sometimes called an elegiac distich.) By the sixteenth century, the definition had narrowed to mean a poem, usually formal, mourning an individual's death. An elegy can also be called a lament, or if you really want to be fancy, a threnody. An elegy not only mourns and praises its subject, it also ideally provides some comfort as well.

An even more narrow version of the form is a pastoral elegy, a style originated by the Greek poets Theocritus and Moschus.

Pastoral elegies portray the poet as a shepherd or goatherd living in an idyllic landscape. The poet is in mourning but usually finds peace or joy by the end of the poem. Although the premise of writing in the voice of a shepherd may seem strange to modern readers, the idea of adopting a persona to address a painful subject is understandable. The idyllic settings for pastoral elegies also provide a sense of peace, evoking an afterlife in paradise. Poets who have used the form include Virgil, Petrarch, Spenser, Shelley, and Arnold.

Who is honored in an elegy depends on the poet. Although often a loved one or friend, some poets address the loss of a public figure, as Walt Whitman did in *When Lilacs Last in the Dooryard Bloom'd*, an elegy on the death of Abraham Lincoln. Poets also are inspired to mark the death of other poets with elegies. Examples of this sub-genre include W.H. Auden's "In Memory of W.B. Yeats" and Percy Bysshe Shelley's elegy for John Keats, "Adonais."

One of the most succinct forms of death poetry is an *epitaph*. Another term with Greek origins, meaning "upon a tomb," an epitaph is a brief verse in remembrance of the dead. As the Greek origins indicate, an epitaph is commonly found on headstones or tombs.

POEMS TO LOVE ABOUT DEATH

Let's take a closer look at a few notable English-language death poems.

"Lycidas" by John Milton

"Lycidas," composed in 1637, is a pastoral elegy. In his introduction, Milton referred to his poem as a monody, which is a Greek poem of mourning presented by one singer. His style mimics the disorientation of grief: he uses irregular stanzas, rhymes, and short lines. At one level, the poem is about Milton mourning the drowning death at the age of twenty-five of his Cambridge University friend Edward King. On another level, Milton's personal loss takes a back seat to the greater loss of all King could have accomplished had he lived, the loss of all that promise. Milton casts King as the shepherd Lycidas and populates the poem with other gods, nymphs, and muses, using imagery that evokes ancient Greece, not seventeenth-century Cambridge. The poem also makes a thinly veiled critique of Anglican priests as ineffective shepherds.

In Memoriam A.A.H. by Alfred, Lord Tennyson

Tennyson's masterpiece was also written in the memory of a Cambridge student lost at a young age. Arthur Hallam, Tennyson's dear friend, was twenty-two when he died. Tennyson wrote the poems over nearly seventeen years, before they were collected and edited for publication in 1850. The 131 lyrics were shaped into three sections, sandwiched by a prologue and an epilogue. The book is a remarkable piece of work that conveys not only Tennyson's intense personal grief but parlays the experience into a wider meditation on faith, love, mortality, and maintaining hope in the worst of times. For a poem about death, it's a surprisingly uplifting work, and concludes with a wedding poem for Tennyson's sister and the promise of a new generation. It gave us this memorable line: "'Tis better to have loved and lost / Than never to have loved at all."

"Do Not Go Gentle Into That Good Night" by Dylan Thomas

Twentieth-century Welsh poet Dylan Thomas did not shy away from writing about death. His collection *Deaths and Entrances* includes many poems written in response to World War II. His most enduring poem, "Do Not Go Gentle Into That Good Night," however, is a poem written while his father was ill, and it anticipates his death. Thomas wrote it in 1947 as a villanelle, a highly structured style of poem. As its title implies, the poem bursts with energy, repeating the title line and "Rage, rage against the dying of the light" multiple times. Thomas looks first at mankind, at men who have lived knowing death will inevitably come but have still not achieved all that they could, before zooming the poem in to portray his dying father and his fierce tears. Although it is a modern poem, Thomas's style is reminiscent of the highly emotional poems of the Romantics.

Villanelle

A villanelle is a nineteen-line poem with five three-line stanzas, followed by a four-line stanza. The first and third lines of the first stanza repeat alternately in the following four stanzas, until the final stanza, when they form the last two lines of the poem as a rhyming couplet.

"Sylvia's Death" by Anne Sexton

Sexton's poem was written in 1963, just six days after her friend and fellow poet Sylvia Plath committed suicide at the age of thirty. The poem, written in free verse, uses short lines that snake their way down the page. This is not a refined, reflective poem on death. It is a confessional scream of pain, a highly personal poem that vividly reveals the shock, anguish, and anger of its author. Sexton herself struggled with thoughts of suicide and death, an obsession she and Plath had bonded over, which is alluded to in the poem. Sexton would take her own life in 1974.

FREE VERSE

Footloose and Fancy-Free

At its most basic definition, free verse is poetry that lacks a measured meter. It is also sometimes referred to by its French name, *vers libre*. Free verse lacks regular meter and line length, relies on natural speech rhythms and grammatical breaks, and may use frequent repetition, parallelism, or alliteration. Although we tend to think of free verse as a modern invention, its roots date back at least as far as the Old Testament of the Bible. Read the long verses that comprise Song of Solomon and the Psalms and you'll quickly see the beauty of the language, even without rhyme and a strict meter. Other early cultures with evidence of free verse in their literature include the Sumerians and Egyptians.

Helpful Terms

Anaphora: Starting a series of lines, phrases, or sentences with the same word or phrase.

Enjambment: A run-on line whose rhythmic movement or sense carries on to the next line.

Parallelism: Using similar grammatical constructions to convey equally important ideas.

Blank Verse: Not to be confused with free verse, blank verse is poetry written in unrhymed iambic pentameter.

More recently, the form was adopted in the late nineteenth century by French poets, most notably Gustave Kahn, who is sometimes credited with inventing the modern use of the form, and Arthur Rimbaud. In America, early practitioners include Walt Whitman and Emily Dickinson. In the twentieth and twenty-first centuries, it has become the dominant poetic form.

FREE-VERSE CHARACTERISTICS

Free verse plays fast and loose with rules—often characterized more by the rules it doesn't follow than by rules it does—so it can be a little tricky to define. Let's take a closer look at some of its forms.

Short Lines: Lines in short-lined free-verse poems can be really short, maybe only a word or two. To avoid meter, the length must be somewhat variable. Some poets will retain entire phrases but others opt for a more jarring effect, by ending a line with an article or preposition.

Long Lines: Walt Whitman was a fan of this style, stretching a line from margin to margin or dropping it down below its beginning with an indented line.

Variable Lines: Possibly the most popular form of free verse, this style keeps a reader on his or her toes, using a variety of lengths in the lines.

Spatial Arrangement and Typography: In a break from poetry's spoken roots, spatial arrangement poems rely on the poem's appearance on the page for meaning. The poet makes deliberate choices about its appearance, making decisions about the arrangement of lines and how white space is used. Line by line, anything goes—a poet may change fonts or type sizes mid-sentence or mid-poem, ignore or overuse punctuation, experiment with capitalization, or insert symbols and numbers into the text.

Unpredictability: Poetry that uses regular rhythm and rhyme can run the risk of becoming boring. Knowing exactly what to expect, line after line, can become tedious for a reader. In free verse, though, unpredictability is the rule. Line lengths may vary, entire sections of poems may abruptly switch styles, and ideas may be left half-finished at the end of a line.

THE APPEAL OF FREE VERSE

So, what's the appeal?

For some readers, free-verse poetry can look undisciplined, even silly. Compare a page of Allen Ginsberg's free verse in "Howl" with a page of Shakespeare's iambic pentameter in *Hamlet*. While both, for a variety of reasons, can be difficult for new readers to understand, the latter at least provides a stability in form and rhyme, which is easily defined as poetry.

For some proponents of free verse, the form removes the artificiality that defines structured poetry. Our lives, our thoughts, our conversations, and our emotions are often messy, nonlinear, and unpredictable. By not tying poems up into tidy packages, free verse can reflect that mess. The result for a reader can be cathartic, a recognition of his or her own reality.

Beauty, too, has a role in free verse. Because it doesn't have to conform to predetermined rhythms or line lengths, it can more naturally mimic our language and conversations. The poem can speed up and slow down at will, just as we do when speaking. By breaking up sentences and lines in unexpected ways, free verse can help us find meaning, forcing us to more closely consider words and how we use them. Enjambment can also create a musical quality that may be pleasing to our ears. Creating white space on a page allows us to pause in our reading, and maybe even provides a moment of reflection before we move onward with the text. When repetition is used in free verse, it can be stirring, lifting our spirits and willing us to keep reading. Free-verse poets can be exacting and precise in their language, carefully selecting just the right noun or verb to convey a sentiment or emotion or to provide an image.

It's not a coincidence that free verse gained popularity in the last century. For the majority of people living in the United States or Great Britain, modern life comes with significantly fewer rules than it did for those living in previous centuries. We have unprecedented freedom to dress as we please, worship as we please, sleep with or marry whom we please, vote as we please, study what we please, and, yes, write what we please. Our culture may not always embrace nonconformity, but it generally allows it. Poets can write in whatever format speaks to them personally and no one gets to tell them no.

For those of you still skeptical about the merits of free verse, keep an open mind. In coming sections, we'll look more closely at the work of individual poets who are gifted at writing in free verse, including Whitman, Ezra Pound, William Carlos Williams, E.E. Cummings, and Sylvia Plath. Each poet rendered the form into a unique expression of his or her own voice, often with great creativity and imagination, not to mention intelligence and wit. All qualities, by the way, they share with the gifted traditional poets from earlier eras we've already studied closely.

WALT WHITMAN (1819–1892)

An American Original

Walt Whitman was an American journalist, essayist, and poet, best known for his *Leaves of Grass* poetry collection, a series of poems that were a work in progress for most of his writing career. Although he was writing during the Victorian era, Whitman's free-verse poetry is emphatically modern, not only in style but in content. His voice is an essentially American voice: forthright, independent, and egalitarian.

A BRIEF CHILDHOOD

Walt Whitman was born on May 31, 1819, on Long Island, New York, although he spent most of his childhood in Brooklyn. His family was not well off. His parents, Walter and Louisa, had nine children and Walter struggled to provide for his family while working as a carpenter and a real estate speculator. Childhood was brief for young Walt. After attending public schools in Brooklyn, he quit by age twelve to begin an apprenticeship in the printing trade. His literary education continued through self-effort, reading the classics and the Bible, and taking advantage of the cultural offerings of New York City.

At twenty-three, after having worked as a printer and a teacher, he embarked on his third career as a newspaper editor. He edited newspapers in both New York, and briefly, New Orleans, but his committed liberal views and antislavery stance eventually damaged his career prospects. Starting in 1850, he spent a few years following in his father's footsteps as a carpenter. He put his suit away, grew a beard, and began to think of himself as a poet.

LEAVES OF GRASS

In 1855, Whitman self-published 1,000 copies of the first edition of *Leaves of Grass*, which contained only twelve poems and a preface. Boldly, Whitman mailed a copy to Ralph Waldo Emerson, a prominent American writer and philosopher best known for his transcendental philosophy. Whitman's moxie paid off: Emerson called his book "the most extraordinary piece of wit and wisdom that America has yet contributed." Emerson wrote an introduction for a later edition.

In 1856, Whitman published a new edition of *Leaves of Grass*, with revisions of the previous poems as well as newcomers. He would continue to revise and issue new, expanded, and rearranged editions for the remainder of his life. The ninth and final edition, published near his death in 1892, held nearly 400 poems. With each new edition, the highly personal poems reflected the changing nature of their aging author. Later editions reveal more of an elder statesman persona and less of the passionate and self-absorbed young poet.

What's special about *Leaves of Grass*? Whitman aspired to nothing less than a new kind of poetry, suitable to the land he lived in. In his preface to the 1855 edition, he wrote "The United States themselves are essentially the greatest poem." Whitman embraced the America of his day. He loved its energy, hustle, and industry as much as its natural landscapes and open spaces. In a nation that prized individualism, Whitman was a natural spokesperson. His work wasn't coy. He displayed unabashed egotism, albeit often tempered with humor. With a wink, he could write, "I dote on myself, there is that lot of me and all so luscious."

Whitman's free-verse style was idiosyncratic by the standards of the day. His poems weren't tidy and neat, with lines marching obediently down the page. They meandered, with stanzas of varying lengths, and occasional lines that dropped and indented a line below before finishing their thought. For a public used to the measured lyrics of Tennyson, Wordsworth, and Keats, Whitman represented at least a puzzle, if not a revolution.

Song of Myself and When Lilacs Last in the Dooryard Bloom'd

These poems, both found within the pages of *Leaves of Grass*, reveal different facets of Whitman's talent and style. *Song of Myself* is a series of fifty-two separate lyrics, which, together, loosely form an epic. The poem plays with the tension of the poet's individuality paired with his sense of belonging to the greater universe. It's densely written and packed with imagery, much of it sexual, and much of that clearly homosexual. In a stream of consciousness, Whitman expresses views on everything from death to equality to the beauty of nature.

Lilacs is a more restrained poem, with more concrete and clear descriptions than *Song of Myself*, although no less emotional. It was written as an elegy after President Lincoln's assassination in 1865 but much of the poem explores the poet's sense of grief, not only for the president, but for the many war dead. The poem becomes an exposition on grief in the universal sense. For several stanzas, he addresses death directly, and warmly, offering a chant of welcome to her, saying "I joyously sing the dead, Lost in the loving floating ocean of thee..." Although in free verse, Whitman gives a bit of structure to the poem by using repeating motifs of lilac, star, and bird.

Picture This

Whitman used an unconventional title page for the 1855 *Leaves of Grass*. Where most books print the author's name, his showed a photograph of the author, dressed in workman's clothes, his hat cocked, and one hand casually slipped into a pocket. Although he included his name in later versions, each edition featured a new photograph. Over the years, Whitman morphed into the heavily bearded, kind-eyed gentleman most modern readers picture when they think of him.

WHITMAN AND THE CIVIL WAR

The US Civil War (1861–1865) profoundly altered the course of Whitman's life, not to mention his nation. Early in the war, his enthusiasm was shown in the rhythmic poem "Beat! Beat! Drums!" His brother George was a Union soldier lightly wounded in 1862. Whitman traveled to the front and nursed him at a hospital for two weeks. Whitman remained a volunteer nurse in Washington, DC, throughout the war, caring for the dying and the wounded. As he witnessed the terrible loss of life caused by the war, his views became decidedly less romantic. He was deeply moved by the soldiers' plight, and angered by the glaring lack of resources to ease their pain or help them heal. Whatever money he made, he funneled it back into the hospitals. He reflects on his wartime experiences eloquently in the poems "The Wound-Dresser" and "Vigil Strange I Kept on the Field One Night."

After the war, he became a clerk in the Department of the Interior, but was fired when he was outed as the author of *Leaves of Grass*, considered an indecent book. Friends rallied to his aid and he found a new placement in the office of the attorney general. In 1873, he suffered a serious stroke and moved to live with his brother in Camden, New Jersey. He was never able to return to DC although he did eventually move into a little house of his own. He died in 1892. Although he received some recognition during his lifetime, especially in Europe, his poetry would not gain widespread appreciation in his beloved United States until the twentieth century.

EMILY DICKINSON (1830–1886)

A Fine American Mind

Emily Dickinson holds a unique place in the American imagination. Remembered for her great talent, she also is closely associated with a half-true/half-imagined myth swirling around her life as a spinster recluse in Amherst, Massachusetts. What we do know for certain is that over the course of her lifetime she quietly produced almost two thousand poems in a distinctive, passionate voice, which merits her placement among the best writers of her generation. Together with Walt Whitman, Dickinson ushered in a new era of poetry in the United States.

THE QUIET LIFE

On December 10, 1830, Dickinson was born into one of Amherst's leading families, that of Edward and Emily Dickinson. Her grandfather had helped found Amherst College, and her father, Edward, was treasurer of the college, as well as an ambitious lawyer. Later in life, he would serve as a US congressman. Every Sunday, Dickinson and her older brother, Austin, and younger sister, Lavinia, would attend services with their family at the local Congregational church. Although Dickinson and her sister were expected to grow up, marry, and manage a household, they were still well educated. Dickinson completed secondary schooling at Amherst Academy, where she took many science classes, and went on to attend Mount Holyoke Female Seminary. She returned home after a year. Like so many details in her life, there are only theories for why she did so, ranging from extreme shyness, her father's request, or because she refused to participate in a Christian revival meeting.

Dickinson lived out the rest of her days in her childhood home, with only occasional outings outside of Amherst, including a two-month trip in 1855 with her sister to Philadelphia and Washington, DC, when her father was a member of Congress. She made her last known trip outside of Amherst in 1865, to Cambridge for medical treatments for an eye disorder.

Dickinson's Literary Influences

According to family members, Dickinson hung up portraits in her bedroom of some of her favorite writers, including Elizabeth Barrett Browning, the novelist George Eliot, and the historian Thomas Carlyle. Her reading tastes also included other British female contemporary writers, including Charlotte and Emily Brontë. Barrett Browning's *Aurora Leigh*, a feminist epic poem about an aspiring poet, was a favorite.

As a girl, she was described as sunny and energetic. But as she aged, shyness took over, to the point where she no longer left the house. Her social life included Austin and his wife, Susan, who lived next door; Lavinia, who lived at home; her parents until their deaths in 1874 and 1882; and perhaps a local friend or two. Through letters, she had a large circle of family and friends. She found a literary mentor in Thomas Wentworth Higginson, an *Atlantic Monthly* editor, who became her pen pal in 1862 and encouraged her to keep writing poetry. At some point, she began wearing all white.

Since her life details are so spare, and her poetry so vibrant, people over the years have invented their own details. Based on letters, she has been connected romantically to the married Rev. Charles Wadsworth of Philadelphia; Benjamin Newton, a student in her father's law office; and even, improbably, her sister-in-law, Susan. She wrote three erotic and highly distressed letters to an unnamed "Master."

Her poetry indicates that she underwent some sort of emotional or mental crisis in her late twenties or early thirties, but whether the cause was a failed love affair or something else has never been determined.

Conflating the poet with the "I" in her poems does not necessarily flesh out her biographical details. Dickinson may have used her rich imagination to compose many of the poems that have been viewed as confessional. When she died in 1886 of chronic nephritis, an inflammation of the kidneys, she took her secrets with her.

POEMS OF GREAT PASSION

Until her death, not even Dickinson's family realized how much writing had consumed her life. She was prolific and versatile, writing eloquently on a variety of topics. Her poetry captures a wide range of observations about the world and her emotional experiences in it, surprising for a woman who was a homebody. Her poems look spare on the page, rarely more than a few four-line stanzas per poem, and typically use an iambic meter. The style is similar to the hymns she would have grown up singing. She was fond of dashes—her verses are riddled with them—and she never titled her work.

Dickinson, in her letters and poems, was gifted at adopting different voices. In her work, we see:

- A feminist who rejects the drudgery of marriage and housework.
- A religious skeptic with a questioning mind who possesses faith but not in step with her Calvinist upbringing.

- A scientist who was a close observer of nature.
- A young woman with sexual and romantic feelings.
- A soul struggling with the deaths of friends and her own mortality.

Her poems can be puzzling and cryptic; their brevity does not mean they are simplistic. Within a short poem, she could share creative metaphors, sharp contrasts, and intense emotions.

Sound Familiar?

Many of Dickinson's poems, or at least lines from them, have taken on iconic status: "Because I could not stop for Death," "'Hope' is the thing with feathers," "I felt a Funeral, in my Brain," and "Tell all the Truth but tell it slant."

LEGACY

Dickinson published fewer than a dozen poems in her lifetime. After her death, her sister Lavinia found the rest, little bundles in hand-stitched books, hidden in a bureau drawer, as well as tucked away in whatever was handy, including old envelopes. A volume published in 1890, compiled and edited by family friend Mabel Loomis Todd, proved a huge success and went through eleven editions in two years. Dickinson liked to revise, often writing several variations of single poems, a habit that has made it hard for scholars to determine a "final" version for publication. It wasn't until 1955 that a thorough and well-regarded edition of her work was published: *The Poems of Emily Dickinson,* edited by Thomas H. Johnson. In 1998, a new version appeared by R.W. Franklin, stripped of many of the editorial changes made to Dickinson's original work over the years.

Her letters, and some of her poems, indicate that she did not seek out fame. Yet, Dickinson became one of the most famous female poets in history. More than one hundred years after her death, she is still one of America's favorite poets.

WILLIAM BUTLER YEATS (1865–1939)

An Irish Patriot

Although he spent nearly two thirds of his life outside of Ireland, William Butler Yeats is an Irish poet whose love of country flows through his poetry. He passionately devoted himself to Irish national art, both in poetry and drama. Writing near the turn of the century, his work is post-Romantic as well as pre-Modern. As an Irishman, he stands near—but apart from—many of his admiring British contemporaries. After his death, poet T.S. Eliot called him "the greatest poet of our time."

LIFE, WORK, AND INFLUENCES

Yeats was born in Dublin in 1865 to the lawyer-turned-painter John Butler Yeats and Susan Pollexfen Yeats. He grew up, not very happily, in Dublin, London, and County Sligo, the home of his mother's wealthy Anglo-Irish family. As a young man, Yeats gravitated to the Celtic Revival, a movement to promote Ireland's cultural heritage in opposition to English influence and rule. Beginning in the eighteenth century, Irish, Scottish, and Welsh writers sought to foster national pride by composing work which drew from their distinctive languages, mythologies, and literary traditions. Although some of the poetry, plays, fiction, and translations sentimentalized the culture, the movement did help preserve and popularize work which might otherwise have been lost. Yeats was influenced greatly by the movement, choosing to integrate Irish folk traditions into his poetry and plays, and would remain a passionate Irishman throughout his life.

He published his first poems in 1885, in the *Dublin University Review*. At the time, he was a student at Dublin's Metropolitan School of Art, although he left art school in 1886. Yeats's earliest poems show a reverence for the Romantic writers, particularly Shelley, but at the urging of Irish patriot and nationalist John O'Leary, Yeats began to research and write about Irish subjects. Reluctantly, he moved with his family to London for several years, a move that proved helpful to his development as a writer. While living there, he found the Rhymers' Club, a group of young poets who critiqued and supported one another. It was also in London, in 1889, where he fell deeply in love with Maud Gonne, a beautiful Irish revolutionary. She became a good friend and confidant for the remainder of his life but rejected his numerous proposals of marriage. Instead, she served as a muse to him and appears in idealized form, in many guises, in his poetry.

Yeats's poetry in the 1890s reflected the aesthetic sensibilities of many of his London peers, including Oscar Wilde. They believed in art for art's sake, a departure from the morality-driven poetry that was popular throughout the Victorian period. Yeats produced some of his most dense and image-rich poetry during this time. In his 1899 poetry collection, *The Wind Among the Reeds*, a few of the poems showed the influence of his increased interest and adherence to mysticism and the occult. Although born into a Protestant family, Yeats would become a religious mystic who rejected the division between Catholics and Protestants that had brutally severed Ireland.

Theater and Rebellion

Yeats spent the first decade of the new century establishing a national theater for Ireland at the Abbey Theatre in Dublin. Founded with Lady Augusta Gregory, the theater was intended to showcase Irish talent. Yeats managed the theater and wrote many of the plays staged there. Writing plays helped him learn how to pare down the flowery, elaborate tone he had used while living in London. Around 1910, Yeats became friends with Modernist poets, including expat American Ezra Pound and T.S. Eliot, and his clear rejection of Romantic styles may also be traced to their influence. His collections, *In the Seven Woods* in 1903, *The Green Helmet and Other Poems* in 1910, and *Responsibilities and Other Poems* in 1914, are populated with tightly crafted poems.

A Vision

Yeats developed a complicated symbolic theory of the universe which he called *A Vision*, first published in 1925 and again in revised form in 1937. Yeats used this mythology as a map of sorts for his later poetry, proving him with a means of exploring the human experience.

In 1916, the Irish Easter Rising, a six-day failed insurrection against the British government by Irish nationalists, rekindled his Irish patriotism. (Among the fifteen executed leaders was the ex-husband of Maud Gonne.) Yeats's poem, "Easter, 1916," was published in 1921 and captured his conflicted feelings about the uprising, but ultimately his respect for the nationalists. After the uprising, Ireland plunged into a war for independence, leading to the establishment of the Irish Free State for twenty-six of Ireland's thirty-two counties in 1921. A brief civil war followed, with violence still smoldering when Yeats took on the potentially dangerous role as a senator of the new Irish Free State in 1922. He served a second term from 1925–1928.

Marriage and Maturity

By that point, Yeats was finally a married man. Both Maud and her daughter, Iseult, had turned down proposals from him in 1916 and 1917. The English socialite Georgie Hyde-Lees said yes, however, and they married in 1917 when she was twenty-five. They had a daughter in 1919 and a son in 1921. Hyde-Lees and Yeats met through occult circles, and she encouraged and collaborated with him in exploration of mystical principles.

Yeats produced some of his best work during the last twenty years of his life. He'd received the Nobel Prize in Literature in 1923 but did not sit back to enjoy his laurels. He used his experiences during the early years of the Irish Free State to great effect in his poetry, especially in the collection *The Tower*, published in 1928. Despite the changes in poetry trends, he stayed true to his own strengths and continued to skillfully use rhymes and structured stanzas in his poems. His poems bubble with energy, even when he rails in them against growing older. Yeats wrote many of his poems on topics central to Ireland, but he infused them with a universality, helping fuel his popularity around the globe.

Yeats died in southern France in 1939, where he had moved because of deteriorating health. His body would have to wait until 1948—after World War II—to be returned to Ireland for his final resting place.

"I will arise and go now, and go to Innisfree,
And a small cabin build there, of clay and wattles made:
Nine bean-rows will I have there, a hive for the honey-bee;
And live alone in the bee-loud glade."

—"The Lake Isle of Innisfree," William Butler Yeats

WAR POETRY

The Good, the Bad, and the Ugly

Poetry expresses some of the best aspects of being human, including our abilities to love, to be brave, and to see beauty in the world around us. Poetry can also take us down into the depths of humanity's worst moments, shining a light on our depravity, our cruelty, and our base instincts.

Poets have been drawn to the subject of war since, well, since poets started writing poems. Remember Homer and his epics about the Trojan War? Some war poems celebrate battle, especially the classical ones, eloquently portraying ideals such as honor, courage, and patriotism. Other poems, particularly in the past couple of centuries, take a critical stance, questioning the carnage, mourning the losses, and weeping for the devastation wrought on people and communities.

Poets in love write love poems, so soldiers must write war poems, right? Yes, no, and maybe. Soldiers have written some of the most highly regarded war poems, but men and women on the home front who never set foot on a battlefield have also written acclaimed war poetry. Journalists form the majority of the "maybe" contingent, witnessing wars firsthand without participating in them.

WORLD WAR I

World War I was a conflict unlike any other in world history, resulting in over sixteen million deaths. For a variety of reasons, World War I produced an extraordinary amount of English-language war

The poetry of the Greek writer Sappho of Lesbos has almost all been lost, and it is known only through quotations from other writers. She wrote about 10,000 lines of poetry, but today we know only 650. In the patriarchal society of ancient Greece, women were not encouraged to participate in the arts, and Sappho was unusual in her poetry writing.

In a painting by the nineteenth-century artist Jean-Baptiste Wicar, the Roman poet Virgil reads his poem *The Aeneid* to the emperor Augustus and his sister and wife. Virgil was greatly influenced by the Homeric epics *The Iliad* and *The Odyssey*. His intention in *The Aeneid* was to create a foundation myth for the Roman people, one that he deliberately linked to Homer's stories of the Trojan War, the most important myth in the ancient world.

Beowulf, the oldest known English language poem, survives in a single manuscript, pictured here, from the eighth century. The manuscript itself was damaged in a fire in 1731 at the Cotton library. That library later became a founding part of the British Library, which holds the manuscript today. The fire obliterated a number of words of the poem, which scholars have tried to reconstruct.

In his great poem *The Divine Comedy*, the poet Dante visits Hell, Purgatory, and Heaven—the first two in the company of the Roman poet Virgil. As a result of this journey, Dante's faith is renewed and he meets the spirit of his beloved, Beatrice, in Heaven. Here, in an engraving by the nineteenth-century artist Gustave Doré, Virgil and Dante encounter souls working their way through Purgatory toward salvation.

Canterbury Cathedral in Canterbury, Kent, England, was a popular pilgrimage site during the Middle Ages. In the second half of the fourteenth century, the poet Geoffrey Chaucer composed a series of "tales" supposedly told by a group of pilgrims traveling there. *The Canterbury Tales* was notable for being one of the first medieval poems written in English rather than in Latin and marked a new stage in the use of English as a poetic language.

Among the most famous Arthurian poems of the Middle Ages was the anonymous *Sir Gawain and the Green Knight*. The poem features the mysterious Green Knight, who at the poem's start enters Arthur's court and volunteers to let any knight strike his head from his shoulders. When Gawain does so, the Green Knight picks up his head and tells Gawain that in a year and a day he must meet the knight and have his own head cut off.

William Shakespeare is regarded by many as the greatest poet in the English language. He invented hundreds of new words, transforming the way people wrote and spoke. His poetry uses powerful images to create a wide range of emotions. Shakespeare's poetic gifts are reflected in the blank verse he used in his plays, but they are particularly evident in his sonnets. Although this is a popular depiction of him, no portrait of him was created during his lifetime.

The violent clashes of armies during the English Civil War (1642–1651), seen in this painting of the Battle of Marston Moor by J. Barker, are thought to have influenced John Milton's epic poem *Paradise Lost* about the downfall of Lucifer and the expulsion of Adam and Eve from Eden.

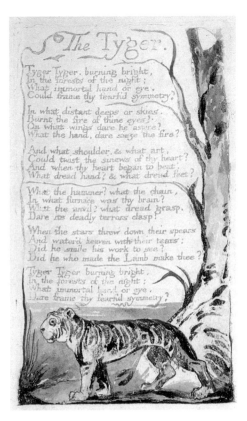

The Romantic poets, who wrote in the last part of the eighteenth and early part of the nineteenth century, often depicted the tension between creativity and order. Poet and artist William Blake illustrated many of his own poems, adding a further layer of meaning to them. Shown here is his depiction of "The Tyger" from his book *Songs of Experience*. Blake sees the tyger contrasting with "The Lamb" in his book *Songs of Innocence*. While the lamb represents innocence and purity, the tyger is both primal ferocity and the artistic fire, which creates its own form of beauty.

Emily Brontë (center), one of the three talented Brontë sisters, wrote poetry in her home in the Yorkshire moors. She was also celebrated for her groundbreaking "anti-romance novel," *Wuthering Heights*, while her sister Charlotte (right) wrote the equally revolutionary novel *Jane Eyre*. Anne (left), the third sister, was the author of the Gothic novel *The Tenant of Wildfell Hall*. The fourth figure in the painting, partially obscured, is Branwell Brontë, the sisters' brother, who painted the picture.

Emily Dickinson lived in relative isolation, and yet her poetic vision turned inward to produce verse that is widely read today. As a result of a national wave of religious reform in 1845, Dickinson became more deeply observant of her Christian faith, although this did not last. Still, it deeply influenced the direction of her poetry, giving it a focus on spiritual matters.

Ezra Pound was notorious both for the unusual quality of his poetry and for the violence of his political views. A translator, editor, and critic, as well as a poet, he worked with many other poets, including T.S. Eliot, W.B. Yeats, and Robert Frost. During the 1930s he lived in Italy, where he openly expressed sympathy for Mussolini's fascists. After World War II, he was arrested and imprisoned in St. Elizabeths Hospital. He was released in 1958.

The Lake Poets, William Wordsworth, Samuel Taylor Coleridge, and Robert Southey, lived and worked in the Lake District of England, in the northwest of the country. Their poetry reflected the surrounding beauties of nature. Buttermere was a principal lake of the area.

Shown here speaking at the inauguration of Bill Clinton in 1993, Maya Angelou was a poet, critic, composer, singer, essayist, playwright, and autobiographer. Rising from a background of poverty, she became a dancer and later decided to concentrate on her writing. Although her most famous work is her autobiography, *I Know Why the Caged Bird Sings*, she also published a number of poetry collections, one of which was nominated for a Pulitzer Prize.

African-American poet Langston Hughes wrote of those in American society who were marginalized and excluded from cultural institutions. His poems, which have been compared to those of Walt Whitman for their free-flowing style, urged Americans to reject racism and warned of the consequences if they did not. In his poem "Harlem," Hughes famously asked, "What happens to a dream deferred? Does it dry up like a raisin in the sun?" He replied with the line, "*Or does it explode?*"

Poetry is largely intended to be read aloud, and poetry readings and "slams" (contests in which the audience votes for their favorite poet) have spread around the world. Here a poet reads at the Badilisha Poetry X-Change, an event held in South Africa, which features poetry from Africa and people of African descent. It helped launch Badilisha Poetry Radio, also based in South Africa, which features more than three hundred African poets.

To many young women in the 1960s and 1970s, poet Sylvia Plath became a symbol of the way women's voices were too often stifled and distorted. She suffered from depression and spent a number of months under psychiatric care after attempting suicide. Later, trapped in an unhappy marriage to poet Ted Hughes, Plath took her own life. Some of Plath's fans have, over the years, tried to chisel the "Hughes" off her gravestone.

poems. England, the United States, Canada, and Australia all sent their best and their brightest off to war. Many soldier-poets were highly educated and well-schooled in the classical traditions, and turned their pens to the subject of the war with such force, gusto, and quantity that the genre of war poetry is now intrinsically linked with this specific war. Among them were Rupert Brooke, Wilfred Owen, and Siegfried Sassoon.

Brooke's war poetry falls in line with the heroic tradition. An established poet and Cambridge graduate, Brooke served early in the war and wrote poems that were highly patriotic and glorified the sacrifices the soldiers were making. His most famous war sonnet, "The Soldier," includes the line "If I should die, think only this of me: / That there's some corner of a foreign field / That is for ever England." Brooke romanticized the war in his poetry, which in turn was used to promote the war effort in Britain. He did not live to see the war's end. Brooke saw combat at Antwerp, but after a series of illnesses, was bitten by an insect and died of blood poisoning while on board a naval ship in Greece. He was twenty-seven.

Gruesome Reality

When Owen and Sassoon enlisted, they also entered the war optimistically. Soon, though, the reality of the physical and emotional tolls of battle profoundly changed their outlook, as well as that of many of their peers. As the war dragged on, with soldiers battling in flooded trenches and mowed down by artillery, gas, and bombs, laudatory poems such as Brooke's soured. Owen and Sassoon hold nothing back regarding their brutal experiences, which are vividly described in searing poems, as well as conveying their eventual antiwar stances. In his poem "Dulce et Decorum Est," Owen turns a line of poetry from Horace on its head, calling it a lie that it is sweet to die for your country. Owen was killed in combat in 1918, a few days before the Armistice. Sassoon survived, publishing not only his own intensely vivid and angry war poems, but editing and publishing those of other soldier-poets.

Poems from this era can be difficult to read because they are so raw in their intensity, yet they often are beautifully crafted. Poets used every literary device in their toolboxes to convey their emotions and mental states, whether they were feeling despair, anger, or disorientation. As a result, their work is still startlingly fresh, despite being a century old.

THE RAVAGES OF WAR

The end of World War I in 1918 didn't mark the end of wars and armed conflicts. Fresh material in the form of World War II, as well as conflicts in Korea, Vietnam, Afghanistan, and Iraq, have moved thousands more poets to address war in verse. Although poets for these modern battles have shown more willingness to question war than earlier generations, there is no single consensus for what role poetry should have in a society at war. The Romantics truly believed their poems should take center stage in debates and decisions at the national level. Today's poets tend to be more modest in their opinions of themselves as national thought leaders. They don't necessarily expect to alter the course of history with their work.

The role of poetry about war continues to be debated. Does it serve any point? Can it be cathartic? Is it moral to glorify war? Should it be used as protest? Should it only be written by those who have seen combat? Or is there room—and a need for—other viewpoints? Much of the war poetry written prior to World War I was written by civilians. During Vietnam, civilians also wrote much of that era's poetry, but as protest, not praise. The US conflicts in Afghanistan and Iraq have been quieter on the poetry front, although there's still plenty of time for more poetry to emerge—by the public, by soldiers, by their families. Each generation must reconcile itself not only with its present, but with its past.

Further Study

The canon of war poetry is vast and diverse. Here are a few from different eras to get you started in your reading:

- "Concord Hymn" (1836)—Ralph Waldo Emerson
- "On Being Asked for a War Poem" (1915)—W.B. Yeats
- "MCMXIV" (1964)—Philip Larkin
- "The Lost Pilot" (1967)—James Tate
- "After Our War" (1974)—John Balaban
- "The Death of the Ball Turret Gunner" (1945)—Randall Jarrell
- "Welcome to Hiroshima" (1985)—Mary Jo Salter
- "Unmentioned in Dispatches" (1991)—Peter Wyton
- "September Songs, A Poem in Seven Days" (2001)—Lucille Clifton
- "Facing It" (2001)—Yusef Komunyakaa

THE MODERNISTS

Out with the Old, In with the New

Artists working in poetry, literature, art, theater, music, and architecture viewed the twentieth century as a clean slate. They rejected not only Victorian-era artistic principles but, in many cases, all artistic precedents. In both Europe and America, poets worked to redefine poetry, seeking new ways of expression and new ways to use language. Modernist poets included Ezra Pound, T.S. Eliot, William Carlos Williams, E.E. Cummings, Langston Hughes, and Marianne Moore.

HISTORY LESSON

The first half of the twentieth century was a period of great change. Two World Wars (1914–1918 and 1939–1945) wracked the globe, as did a Great Depression (1929–1939). Technological advances, many brought about because of the wars, included: shifts in transportation to widespread use of automobiles and airplanes, improvements in communications with the advent of the telephone, expansion of electrical power usage, and the development of nuclear weapons and atomic power. Philosophy, political theories, and scientific advancements all contributed to the changing intellectual atmosphere. Ideas introduced in the nineteenth century had taken root and began to have profound repercussions for modern life, including Darwin's *On the Origin of Species*, first published in 1859, with its radical findings that humans and all of nature evolved over time.

Karl Marx's revolutionary nineteenth-century *The Communist Manifesto* and *Capital: A Critique of Political Economy* functioned as modern guides to socialism and an examination of capitalist economies. Philosopher Friedrich Nietzsche's ideas— including declaring that "God is dead"—took hold among a new generation of philosophers and artists. Sigmund Freud's concepts of the human subconscious, described in *The Interpretation of Dreams* in 1899, inspired many writers to explore new forms of creativity. Albert Einstein blew everyone's minds with his general theory of relativity in 1915.

When exactly the period covered by the Modernists begins and ends is debated. Roughly, the Modernist poets were producing work beginning at the very end of the nineteenth century on through to the 1950s. In literary terms, post-Modernism took over at that point, although many contemporary poems are still composed in Modernist style.

CHARACTERISTICS OF MODERNIST POETRY

Modernist poets rejected the past with gusto. They opposed traditional styles. Instead of working to imitate or perfect well-established forms—the goal of so many of their poetic predecessors—the Modernists wanted to experiment with and manipulate those forms. Often, their experimentations shattered the original form, then picked up the pieces and put them back together in ways nearly unrecognizable from the original. Free-verse style grew in popularity.

Pessimism and despair are frequent themes in Modernist poetry. Poets lost their sense of shared values in society and instead viewed the world as chaotic. To compensate for the unreliability of the wider world, the interior life of the poet took precedence over external concerns.

Aesthetics changed too. Flowery language was out; concise language was in. Rather than using many lines to expound on the beauty of nature, Modernists preferred to boil the descriptions down to their essentials, letting readers find meaning as much in what *wasn't* said as what was said.

Symbolism

Symbolism is when a term or image represents or stands for an abstract meaning or idea. Although the definition sounds a bit like a metaphor, where one thing is compared to another, symbolism reaches for a deeper meaning and representation. In a metaphor, the connection between two things is clear; with symbolism, it's not so obvious. As a literary device, it was used frequently to great effect by Modernist poets who played with the inherent ambiguity symbols provide to a poem.

In late nineteenth-century France, a symbolist poetry movement emerged that emphasized a highly personal form of expression as the aim of art. Writers used carefully chosen words in their poetry to help evoke—and act as symbols of—their deeper emotions. In some uses, the symbols were also intended to be a bridge between the material and spiritual worlds. The French symbolists' concepts and poetry influenced many twentieth-century American and British poets. William Butler Yeats is often considered a symbolist poet. T.S. Eliot was heavily influenced by the movement as well. See his poem "Burnt Norton" as an example.

The Modern Long Poem

Traditionally, long poems, or epics, tried to synthesize the beliefs and values of an entire culture. The Modern long poem, however, spoke for a society that no longer had a unified culture, causing the poet to insert more of his own interpretations and emotions into the poetry. Whitman's *Song of Myself* is an early example. T.S. Eliot's *The Waste Land* is the most well-known Modernist example; others include Edgar Lee Masters's *Spoon River Anthology*, Ezra Pound's *The Cantos*, William Carlos Williams's *Paterson,* and H.D.'s *Trilogy*.

Poetry Magazines

Many Modernist poets were nourished by their affiliation with literary magazines, which helped to fuel and publicize the new movement. In 1914, Margaret Anderson founded *The Little Review* in Chicago and published poets Ezra Pound and E.E. Cummings, among many, until the magazine folded in 1929. Also in Chicago, Harriet Monroe launched *Poetry: A Magazine of Verse* in 1912 and featured many world-renowned poets. The magazine continues to be a leading poetry journal.

RELATED MOVEMENTS

Although the Modernists were the most prominent poetic movement to emerge in the early twentieth century, they were not the only kids on the block, so to speak. Poets, writers, and artists experimented with many artistic philosophies during this period, some overlapping with, and some functioning in direct opposition to Modernism. We'll discuss two more important movements, Imagism and the Harlem Renaissance, in subsequent sections.

Dada

The Dada literary and artistic movement was started in Zurich in 1916 by Tristan Tzara, a Romanian poet and essayist, and had run its course by 1923. Created in response to World War I, the Dada movement took direct aim at traditional art and philosophy, arguing that they should be destroyed and replaced with deliberate nonsense. The term *Dada* is a made-up word and reflects the anarchy its proponents wished to see artists practice. They envisioned total freedom as artists.

Surrealism

Surrealism developed in 1924 in Paris as an outgrowth of Dadaism. Influenced in part by Freud's research, Surrealists stressed the unconscious, valued art produced from dreams, and rejected rational thought. Artists used hypnotism and automatic writing to unleash their imaginations. It was primarily a European movement until after World War II, when it began to influence American poets, including Robert Lowell, Robert Bly, and James Wright.

The Movement

In the 1950s, a group of British poets became known for their conservatism, formal poems, and wit. Adherents included Kingsley Amis, Philip Larkin, and Donald Davie. They were anti-Modernists, in the sense that they preferred a compressed, not fragmented, style of poetry. Their poems displayed intelligence and humor and often used a narrative style.

EZRA POUND (1885–1972)

Modernist Ringleader

Ezra Pound was a ringleader for the Modernist movement. He was a renowned poet, but also a translator, an editor, a critic, a mentor, an innovator, and a tastemaker for an entire generation of poets. His life story is marred by his support of fascism during World War II.

LEADER OF THE PACK

Pound was born in 1885 in the mining town of Hailey, Idaho, to Homer Loomis Pound and Isabel Weston. When he was still very small, the family of three moved to Pennsylvania. Pound grew up in a middle-class neighborhood near Philadelphia. He was educated at Hamilton College and the University of Pennsylvania, where he became friends with William Carlos Williams. He moved to Europe before completing a PhD from the latter university.

In 1908, Pound moved to Venice, Italy, and self-published his first collection of poems, *A Lume Spento*. He lived in London from 1908 to 1920, then in Paris until 1924, where he established his reputation as a poet. Pound was a fan of Robert Browning and W.B. Yeats, who became a friend in London, but he was highly critical of other established English poets. He found their style too emotional and their language arcane. He disliked forced metric and preferred poetry that sounded like everyday speech.

Influential Aesthetic

Pound held several influential editing positions while in London. At various points, he was the foreign editor of *Poetry* magazine as well as the London editor of *The Little Review*. He used his positions to help shape the careers and work of other poets, setting clear guidelines for the poetry he preferred. As a critic for many publications, he advocated for his aesthetic and helped promote his favorite poets, including T.S. Eliot. Pound was responsible for the final edits and cuts to Eliot's *The Waste Land*, considered one of the finest Modernist poems. He also worked closely with Yeats, Robert Frost, D.H. Lawrence, H.D. (Hilda Doolittle), E.E. Cummings, and Ford Madox Ford. Pound also helped launch the careers of American writer Ernest Hemingway and Irish novelist James Joyce, whose novel *Ulysses* was partially serialized in *The Little Review*.

Over the course of his career, Pound published many collections of poetry as well as criticism and essays. He liked the dramatic lyric form, and insisted the "I" in many of his poems was a character and not necessarily him. His lyric poem *Hugh Selwyn Mauberley*, published in 1920, evaluated British culture from the point of view of a British critic-poet. Pound also worked in translation, interpreting early Chinese poems. He worked extensively on a fragmented series of poems called *The Cantos*. The epic collection is more than 800 pages long and serves as a wide-ranging, encyclopedic survey of Pound's political and historical interests, ranging from ancient Greece and China to revolutionary America. Portions had been published during his lifetime, between 1917 and 1946, but the ambitious project was never completed.

Political Views

It's not possible to talk about Pound's legacy without including his affiliation with fascism. Pound moved to Italy in 1924 and remained there throughout World War II. During the war, he made a series of radio broadcasts in which he expressed fascist and anti-Semitic views and chastised President Roosevelt. The US government interpreted his views as treasonous and after the war ended he was imprisoned near Pisa by the occupying American troops. Deemed mentally unfit for a trial, he was placed in St. Elizabeths Hospital in Washington, DC, where he remained for more than a decade. While in the hospital, he was awarded the prestigious Bollingen Prize for Poetry (a literary prize given to poets for either the best new work for two years or for lifetime achievement) for *The Pisan Cantos*, written while incarcerated in Pisa and published in 1948. (*The Pisan Cantos* are a portion of his larger *Cantos* work.) He was not released until 1958, after Robert Frost and other poets had organized a campaign for his freedom. He lived quietly in Italy until his death in 1972.

Sestina

A sestina is a poem with six stanzas. It uses six end words woven in a pattern throughout the poem and finishes with three lines containing all six of the words. The final lines are called an envoi: three of the end words appear at the end of the lines and three of the end words are distributed, one each, within the three lines. The form was developed in France by troubadours. Pound was a fan of the form. In a book of literary criticism, *The Spirit of Romance*, Pound called the sestina: "a thin sheet of flame folding and infolding upon itself."

IMAGISM

Pound was a founder of Imagism, a school of English and American poetry that flourished between 1909 and 1918. Pound created the movement with fellow Londoners T.E. Hulme, a poet and critic, and F.S. Flint, a poet. Hulme was an advocate for free-verse poetry with concise images as a reversal of the Romanticism found in nineteenth-century poems. They formalized their ideas on poetry by publishing their Imagism principles in 1913, which included three poetic goals: direct treatment of "the thing," using only words that contribute to the presentation, and composing in the sequence of a musical phrase. For inspiration, in addition to Greek, Latin, and biblical poetry, they looked at poetic traditions outside of Western culture, including Chinese and Japanese forms. Pound admired the sparse, direct style of haiku. Pound's poem "In a Station of the Metro" is just two lines long but is the quintessential Imagist poem.

Other Imagist poets include H.D., J.G. Fletcher, and Amy Lowell. Lowell met with Pound and his fellow Imagists several times in London before becoming the leader of the movement in America, much to the consternation of Pound, who believed Lowell was diluting the original movement with looser rules. She collected and published three anthologies titled *Some Imagist Poets* (1915–1917). Pound distanced himself from what he called "Amygism," going so far as to rename Imagism "Vorticism" and redefine an image as a vortex.

Although short-lived, Imagism played a role in helping to develop later movements, including Objectivism, whose leading figure was William Carlos Williams, and Projectivism, which is closely associated with the Black Mountain poets.

T.S. ELIOT (1888–1965)

Pushing Boundaries

Thomas Stearns Eliot was born in St. Louis, Missouri, into a displaced New England family in 1888. His grandfather, William Greenleaf Eliot, was a Harvard Divinity School graduate who helped establish Washington University; his father, Henry, was a successful businessman; and his mother, Charlotte, was a poet, schoolteacher, and social worker. Even as a child, he loved poems and published several. At Harvard, he majored in philosophy and was an editor of *The Harvard Advocate*, the university's undergraduate art and literary magazine. He became a critic of Romanticism, while a student, under the tutelage of his professor Irving Babbitt.

In 1914, when Eliot was a graduate student in philosophy at Harvard, he was given a fellowship to study in Germany and at Oxford in England. He stayed on in England, teaching school briefly before moving into a banking position during World War I. He married Vivienne Haigh-Wood in 1915. (The unhappy marriage ended with Vivienne's death seventeen years later.) In 1917, he became assistant editor of *The Egoist*, a magazine featuring Modernist writers, and in 1922, founded and edited *The Criterion*, a literary magazine that continued until 1939. In 1925, he left banking to become an editor at Faber and Faber, where he stayed for the rest of his career.

Symbolism in Poetry

As Eliot began to move in literary circles, he made the acquaintance of poet and critic Ezra Pound. Pound's friendship was pivotal in establishing Eliot as a prominent Modernist poet. Pound was a mentor and editor to Eliot and gave him his first real break, arranging for Eliot's poem "The Love Song of J. Alfred Prufrock" to be published in *Poetry* magazine in June 1915. Later, Pound would help revise and edit *The Waste Land*, Eliot's most celebrated work.

Like Pound, Eliot was influenced by the Metaphysical poets as well as the French symbolists. He helped to make symbolism popular in poetry. His own recurrent symbols included childhood, sexuality, Christianity, and nature. Eliot adopted free verse as his primary style. He viewed the world as complex and complicated and wanted the language of his poems to replicate that variety. It doesn't always make for easy reading, and even admirers of Eliot can find his poetry difficult to wade through. For many readers, the effort is worth it to glean Eliot's perspective on society and to enjoy his precise use of language.

Eliot was critical of modern Western culture in *The Waste Land* and *The Hollow Men* (1925). After Eliot's conversion to the Anglican Church in 1927, his work moved in a more positive, optimistic direction with *Ash Wednesday* in 1930, with its exploration of faith. *Old Possum's Book of Practical Cats* (1939) was light verse originally intended for children. The book became one of Eliot's most popular, and was the source material for Andrew Lloyd Webber's 1981 musical *Cats*. His book of poems, *Four Quartets*, published in 1943, is similar in style to *The Waste Land* but is more meditative and religious, with more structure than its predecessor.

"The Love Song of J. Alfred Prufrock"

When Pound first sent "The Love Song of J. Alfred Prufrock" to *Poetry* editor Harriet Monroe, she resisted publishing it because she didn't think the piece was poetry. The free-verse poem is rich with images, many beautiful, although the narrator seems to despise beauty. It's a dramatic monologue whose "slightly bald" narrator is an anti-Romantic speaker who adopts a dry tone. Prufrock is self-obsessed and although he claims to seek love, his quest is hopeless.

Extraordinary Influence

Eliot was also a prolific critic, editor, and playwright, and his work in those fields is almost as highly regarded as his work as a poet. He received many accolades over the course of his career, including the 1922 Dial Award and the 1948 Nobel Prize for Literature. He had extraordinary influence as a man of letters for his time. His peak popularity was in the 1920s. He was not universally loved, however, with his avant-garde work attracting more than its share of criticism. Some of it was personal: he adopted an almost prissy persona of a proper English gentleman—he had become a British citizen in 1927—which rubbed some people the wrong way. By the 1950s, his writing style had fallen out of favor both by poets pushing poems in new directions and by those returning to the traditional forms Eliot had rejected. Eliot, though, is still considered one of the twentieth century's most influential poets for the solid foundation he provided during a pivotal time in English-language poetry. Eliot remarried in 1957 to Valerie Fletcher. He died in London in 1965.

Verse Drama

Eliot also used verse to compose plays. He steered clear of the Elizabethan blank verse favored by Shakespeare in favor of a new style of verse of his own devising. He strove for a natural rhythm that would be appealing to modern audiences, with most lines containing four strong beats. He published *Murder in the Cathedral* in 1935, *The Family Reunion* in 1939, and *The Cocktail Party* in 1949. For the latter, he won the 1950 Tony Award for Best Play.

THE WASTE LAND

Eliot published *The Waste Land* in 1922. The poem created immediate waves—the ripples are still coming in to shore—and its publication is touted as a key moment in the Modernist movement. The poem approaches the subject of Western civilization with a profound pessimism and distaste.

Eliot wrote and edited *The Waste Land* during a difficult time in his life, when he was struggling with a heavy workload as a banker, a disintegrating marriage, and financial stress. It was published in several forms, first in Eliot's magazine *The Criterion*, then in the American magazine *The Dial*, and then as a book.

The Waste Land is written in free verse and is broken into five chapters of uneven length. Pound's influence is evident in Eliot's use of clear, precise images throughout the poem. (Eliot acknowledged Pound by dedicating the poem to him.) By design, it's a difficult poem to describe. It is fractured in its form, dreamlike in its randomness, and it jumps from subject to subject almost by the line, with many obscure literary and cultural references. What pulls it together is an overall sense of disillusionment with modern, post–World War I life. The poem was both a prize and a puzzle to critics and readers. Some reveled in the imagery and found the form exhilarating and a perfect depiction of the difficulty of the times. Others dismissed it as a ridiculous piece of work. It is now considered a landmark publication for Modern poetry.

MARIANNE MOORE (1887–1972)

The Quiet Modernist

In 1968, poet Marianne Moore threw the opening pitch of the baseball season at Yankee Stadium. She was eighty-one and that rarest of late twentieth-century creatures: a beloved American poet. Moore was a Modernist who, as a young woman, ran with the T.S. Eliot/Ezra Pound/H.D./William Carlos Williams crowd. With time, she accumulated accolades, as well as fame, winning many of the highest honors poets can receive, including a Guggenheim Fellowship (1945), the Bollingen Prize (1951), a Pulitzer Prize (1952), and a National Book Award (1952).

A QUIET BEGINNING

Moore began life in Kirkwood, Missouri, in 1887. Her father wasn't really in the picture: he'd had a mental breakdown and was committed to an asylum when she was a baby. When still very young, Moore's mother, Mary, moved her and her older brother, John Warner, in with Moore's grandfather, a Presbyterian minister. In 1894, after her grandfather's death, they moved to Carlisle, Pennsylvania. Moore was a good student who attended Bryn Mawr, where she published poems in the campus literary magazine. She became good friends with classmate and fellow poet H.D.

After graduating in 1909, Moore took business classes and ended up teaching at a commercial college for four years. She was writing, though, and began publishing her poems in respected journals. Moore had always been very close with her mother, and in 1918, they moved to New York City. They would live in numerous small apartments in Greenwich Village and Brooklyn, often sharing a bed, until her mother died in 1947. Her mother was an active participant in Moore's literary life, editing and critiquing her work.

The Edsel

Moore was contacted by the Ford Motor Company in 1955 to name a new model of car. Moore approached the task with a sense of whimsy. Her suggestions included The Resilient Bullet, Pastelogram, Mongoose Civique, Utopian Turtletop, and Turcotinga. Ford rejected her ideas in favor of the Edsel, named for Henry Ford's son. Both the car and the name were flops.

In New York, Moore continued experimenting with poetic forms and fell in with a social crowd that included Williams, Wallace Stevens, and other emerging Modernist poets. Without Moore's knowledge, her friend H.D published a collection of her poetry, titled *Poems*, in London in 1921. An expanded edition, *Observations*, was published with Moore's consent in 1924. After winning the prestigious Dial Award for *Observations*, Moore went on to become the New York literary magazine's editor from 1925 until it folded in 1929. At *The Dial*, Moore critiqued and edited many of the top writers and poets of the day, including Ezra Pound and James Joyce, among others. Her tastes were sometimes criticized as being prudish: for instance, she found Joyce's *Finnegans Wake* to be too crass.

PRECISE STYLE

Moore wrote very few poems during her editing years but returned to publishing in 1935 with *Selected Poems*, which included an introduction of praise by T.S. Eliot. The book was an artistic, but not commercial, success. One of its most famous poems is called "Poetry," which opened with the line: "I, too, dislike it: there are things that are important beyond all this fiddle."

By that point, Moore had developed a distinctive voice and style. Unlike some of her peers, she was optimistic about humanity, and her work tends to lack the desolate themes that haunt her contemporaries. She was known for having far-reaching and diverse intellectual interests, which were on display in the many topics she explored in her poems. Often, she'd quote directly from her literary—and nonliterary—sources in her poems, a quirk that came to be closely associated with her style. Harkening back to her college biology classes, she loved animals and made frequent allusions to the natural world in her poems. Sports were also a frequent topic. She is sometimes considered an Imagist, like her friend H.D., because she boiled down her poems to essential elements, often with clean, crisp descriptions of tangible things.

Moore was a pioneer in using the first line of her poem as a title. Poems titled this way can seem to start in the middle of a sentence, forcing any readers who skipped the title to backtrack. The technique is also a form of enjambment, creating an extra space—in essence, a pause—separate from the stanza structure. She wrote in free verse but was skilled at using natural rhythms of English language to form graceful, flowing poems. As she aged, her form loosened and her poetry became more playful.

Many consider two of Moore's finest volumes to be *What Are Years*, published in 1941, and *Nevertheless*, in 1944. She chose to rigorously edit her previously published poems and publish them again, but readers and critics sometimes find the edited versions to be too extreme in their brevity. In the 1950s, her poems frequently appeared in *The New Yorker*, and she continued to publish poetry collections into the 1960s.

Syllabic Meter

Accents and lengths of syllables don't matter in syllabic meter: all that counts is the number of syllables. This form of meter is common in French and Japanese poetry but is relatively rare in English. Modernist poets such as Marianne Moore experimented with the style, however, which provided a kind of order to free verse. A syllabic poem may have the same number of syllables in each of its lines or it may use a repetitive stanza form in which the first line of each stanza has the same syllabic count, but subsequent lines may differ. In Moore's poem "The Fish," she uses a syllabic pattern of 1-3-9-6-8.

These days, Moore's name may not register with the general public the way, say, Eliot or Pound might, but her legacy among poets is still well regarded. She was a close friend and mentor to poet Elizabeth Bishop, who met her in 1934, when Bishop was still a student at Vassar. Bishop's style of writing was similar to Moore's in her pursuit of accuracy in her poetry. Sylvia Plath also cited Moore as an influence. Several new books of Moore's poetry and biographies in the last several years indicate interest in her may be on the rise again.

Moore became increasingly eccentric as she aged and was known for appearing in New York in a tricorn hat and cape. Her fondness of baseball and boxing matches was renowned. She even met with Muhammad Ali for a publicity stunt where they co-wrote a poem. She died on February 5, 1972, after a series of strokes over a period of several years.

E.E. CUMMINGS (1894–1962)

Punctuation Schmunctuation

Edward Estlin Cummings was a Modernist poet, essayist, playwright, and painter. He published twelve volumes of poetry over the course of his life, noted for their style, including a disregard for punctuation, as much as for their substance. Somewhat surprisingly, he achieved widespread popularity for a poet among the general reading public and is still a well-known poet.

EARLY ROOTS

Cummings was born in Cambridge, Massachusetts, to Edward Cummings, a Unitarian minister, and Rebecca Haswell Clarke, who descended from a long line of American writers and intellectuals. Cummings began writing poetry from a young age and also loved to draw. He attended the Cambridge Latin School.

At Harvard, he studied literature and received a thorough grounding in the classics for his BA and MA degrees. His college-era poetry, written in free verse, reflects his interest in Modernist and Imagist poets, including Ezra Pound and Amy Lowell.

As a young man, Cummings moved to Greenwich Village in New York City. World War I interrupted his plans for an artistic life of painting and writing poetry. Although a pacifist, in 1917 he enlisted in the Ambulance Corps and was sent first to Paris, and then to the front. Cummings wrote letters home that were critical of the war. The letters were flagged by French censors as suspicious, and he was consequently placed in a detention facility awaiting a judicial commission. He spent three months there, imprisoned in a large room with many others under poor conditions, before he was released and sent to New York in 1918. Once home, he was drafted into the army and spent the rest of the war at Fort Devens in Massachusetts. In the early 1920s, he returned to Paris to study art and became acquainted with other Modernist poets and painters, including Pound and Hart Crane.

Cummings was married three times. He and his first wife, Elaine Orr, married in 1924, but the marriage was brief. They had already had a daughter, Nancy, born in 1919 while Elaine was married to another man. When Cummings and Orr divorced, he lost legal rights to his daughter. A second marriage, in the late 1920s, to Anne Barton, was also brief. Three was a charm, though, and Cummings's final marriage to Marion Morehouse, an actress, model, and photographer, in the early 1930s lasted until his death in 1962.

A NEW TAKE ON PUNCTUATION

Cummings's first book was *The Enormous Room,* a fictionalized, oddly cheerful version of his time in detention in France published in 1922. The book was praised internationally. His first book of poems, *Tulips and Chimneys*, came out in 1923. Cummings had difficulty finding a publisher for the book, which contained poems with sexual content that he had written more than three years earlier. The volume includes only 66 of the 152 poems. More of the rejected poems made it into the collections *XLI Poems* and *&*, in 1925. He published again in 1926, with a volume called *is 5*. Cummings's characteristic manipulation of punctuation and typography was on full display, especially in the later volumes as publishers became more comfortable printing his unconventional poems. That year, he won the prestigious Dial Award, which came with a $2,000 prize that supported him for two years and greatly raised his profile as a poet.

His style could flummox early readers and writers alike, with critics calling his poems ugly and fragmentary and cringing at his spelling and syntax. Others recognized his avant-garde efforts as a revelatory change in the way poems could be composed. His style may have seemed odd to some readers, but it was not random. He meticulously crafted his poems and did not entirely abandon conventions such as rhyme. His poems were sometimes arranged like art on a canvas, with the words and lines spaced and stretched out to fill a page, or mashed into one another. The results are challenging, but Cummings was deliberately altering the way readers experienced his poems. He created a sense of spontaneity on the page and a sense of modern reality not portrayed in formally composed poems. His goal was not just to alter readers' view of poetry, but of life.

Cummings celebrated the individual in his poetry (and prose) and used language to show the beauty of nonconformity. He often mocked modern society and its restrictions on language and thought. He wasn't entirely at odds with mainstream tastes, though. Although he wrote using unconventional styles, his lyric poems also covered conventional poetic topics such as love, childhood, animals, and nature. His early love poetry is praised for its sensuousness and revealing, honest portrayal of physical love. Later, his love poems became more focused on the spiritual aspects of love.

In 1931, Cummings spent a month touring Russia, meeting with artists and writers. In 1933, he published *EIMI*, an idiosyncratic journal of his trip. Visiting Russia disabused him of his socialist views— he was horrified by the reality of life for citizens in communist

Russia—and that break is evident in *EIMI*, which also used the experimental typography Cummings displayed in his poetry.

e e cummings

Cummings's commitment to nonconformity extended to his own name. He occasionally wrote his byline as "e e cummings," humbly rejecting capitalization in the same way he sometimes used "i" for "I" in his poems. Some publishers chose to use the noncapitalized version for the author's name on books but the practice was debated—Cummings never changed his legal name, as rumored—and derided by his widow, Marion Morehouse.

Popularity

Cummings remained in Greenwich Village for the 1930s through the 1950s and stayed at the center of experimental arts throughout that period. Later books include *ViVa* in 1931, *no thanks* in 1935, which were two of his most popular volumes, as well as *50 Poems* in 1940 and *Xaipe* in 1950. The poetry he published beginning in the 1940s was slightly more conventional, with Cummings using more regular poetic forms. In 1957, he was given the Bollingen Prize. Cummings was widely read by the American public and at the time of his death was second in popularity only to Robert Frost. He was popular on the literary circuit and gave many readings. His last book of poems, *95 Poems*, came out in 1958. A posthumous collection, *73 Poems*, was printed in 1963.

Cummings died in 1962 at his summer home, Joy Farm in New Hampshire, after suffering a stroke.

WILLIAM CARLOS WILLIAMS (1883–1963)

The Physician Poet

You probably know the poem. The one with the red wheelbarrow. And some chickens. When *Literary Hub* compiled a list of the most anthologized poems in the past twenty-five years, guess which poem topped the list? "The Red Wheelbarrow" by William Carlos Williams. It's a great poem, but "The Red Wheelbarrow" is only the tip of the iceberg when it comes to getting to know Williams as a poet. Despite spending most of his life in Rutherford, New Jersey, Williams was closely connected to the inner circle of poets who dominated the Modernist movement in the twentieth century's first half, not to mention serving as a mentor and inspiration to the Beat poets who dominated the century's mid-years.

A NEW JERSEY BOY

Williams was born in 1883 in Rutherford, New Jersey, to an English father and a Puerto Rican mother who encouraged his interest in the arts. Williams didn't connect with poetry, though, until he was a student at Horace Mann High School in New York City, where teachers inspired him to use his creativity. His parents didn't see poetry as a good career prospect, and pushed Williams to enroll as a medical student at the University of Pennsylvania.

In Philadelphia, Williams found more than classes on anatomy and biology. In his first year of medical school, he found a lifelong friend in the poet Ezra Pound, an undergraduate studying Romance languages. Pound's friendship opened up a new world for Williams, who had arrived with a fondness for the Romantic poet John Keats, introducing him to new ways of thinking about poetry. Pound welcomed him into his artistic circle, including the poet Hilda Doolittle, and to a free-spirited ethos that contrasted greatly with Williams's quiet and restricted upbringing. While Pound espoused the literary life, Williams continued on his path toward becoming a pediatrician, earning his MD in 1906.

Wearing Two Hats

Williams published his first book of poetry, *Poems*, in 1909, but the style was old-fashioned compared to the work he would produce later. His next book, *The Tempers*, in 1913, embraced many of the tenets of Imagism, the new school of minimalist poetry that Pound was leading from London, where he had moved after university. The two had been corresponding, and Pound helped arrange for the publication. In 1917, Williams published his third volume of poems, *Al Que Quiere!* The book showed his commitment to Imagist ideals.

After his residency, Williams returned to New Jersey, married Florence "Flossie" Herman in 1912, and practiced medicine as a pediatrician for forty years. He maintained a thriving practice while building a parallel career as a poet and often used his day-to-day experiences as material for his poems. Williams developed a desire to create poetry that was distinctly American and would capture the rhythms of the voices he heard every day in his practice. He didn't want to sound like an English poet. Playing with this idea began moving him away from Pound's aesthetic. His willingness to experiment was demonstrated in the 1920 publication *Kora in Hell: Improvisations*, an unusual collection of prose-poem forms and musings from a notebook he had used to record daily observations. The Pound club was not impressed.

It was Williams's turn to not be impressed when, two years later, T.S. Eliot's *The Waste Land* was published. *The Waste Land* took poetry in a different direction than Williams thought he and the other Modernists had been headed, and the praise poets poured onto Eliot irritated him. He wanted poetry to be rooted in the local, not with the intellectual scholarly references that littered *The Waste Land*. Williams's next collection, *Spring and All*, published in 1923, contained experimental poetry and prose. Unlike Eliot, who saw only despair in modern civilization, Williams saw room for imagination, for poetry, to make a real difference in the world. The book was largely ignored.

Variable Foot

Williams coined the term *variable foot*. A variable foot can contain any number of syllables, all adding up to a single beat. In practice, they don't necessarily take up the same amount of time per beat, but the concept gave Williams a way to give a metrical explanation for his free verse. He paired the idea with his concept of a triadic line—poetry composed in sets of three descending lines. Read Williams's poem "Asphodel, That Greeny Flower" for an example.

After *Spring and All,* Williams took a ten-year hiatus from publishing poetry, although he continued writing, publishing short stories, prose, and novels. Fame was elusive for Williams. His patients, and most of the inhabitants of Rutherford, had no idea he was a poet. He didn't gain a consistent following until the late 1940s, after he had been writing for more than twenty years.

PATERSON

Paterson is the work that ultimately established Williams's reputation as a leading poet. The five-volume epic poem was published first as individual volumes between 1946 and 1958, and all together in 1963. He put his theories on grounded poetry into practice by centering the poems on the New Jersey town of Paterson. The city, embodied by a symbolic man of the same name, takes on a mythic quality in the poem, as Williams explores its history, geography, and people. Like Williams, the character of Paterson is seeking a new American language. Not all of the poem is poetry—Williams used a collage format to include prose items such as letters and newspaper reports.

The book's success garnered him an invitation to become the Consultant in Poetry to the Library of Congress, the role now called the poet laureate. He originally deferred due to health concerns. In 1952, he was ready to take up the post but rumors circulating that he was a communist caused the offer to be withdrawn, much to his disappointment.

The Next Generation

By that point, Williams had collected his own coterie of acolytes, many of whom were Beat poets. Robert Lowell, Allen Ginsberg, Denise Levertov, and others found Williams's austere style enticing, and he served as a mentor and editor to another generation of poets. Despite suffering a bad stroke in 1952, Williams continued to write and publish prose books and poems throughout the 1950s. His poetry collections, *The Desert Music and Other Poems*, *Journey to Love*, and *Pictures from Brueghel and Other Poems*, were praised by critics for their maturity and beauty. The latter won him a posthumous Pulitzer Prize in 1963. Sadly, Williams had passed away in March of that year.

W.H. AUDEN (1907–1973)

Tradition and Modernity

Wystan Hugh Auden was born in York, England, into a middle-class family. Shortly after his birth, his family moved to Birmingham, where his father was a physician and professor of public health at the University of Birmingham and his mother was a nurse and ardent Anglican. Auden attended Christ Church, Oxford. He started out on a science scholarship but finished his degree studying English. While there, he became good friends with the poets C. Day Lewis, Stephen Spender, and Louis MacNeice.

Auden's friends at Oxford formed an informal group known as the "Oxford Group." They produced poetry that reflected their left-wing tendencies and interest in Marxism and Freud. Auden wrote about the social and political issues of his day, including poverty, unemployment, and war. Auden's style was succinct, sometimes terse, but almost always eloquent. He also appreciated Anglo-Saxon and Old English poetry, and its influence is visible in his early poems, especially in his use of alliteration.

Spender published Auden's first collection, *Poems,* in 1928 in a handpress edition of forty-five copies. T.S. Eliot was a fan and advocated for *Poems* to be reissued in revised form in 1930 by Faber and Faber, where Eliot was an editor. The publication launched Auden's career. His second collection of poems, *The Orators*, was published in 1932 and examined postwar British society. It was followed by *The Dance of Death* in 1933, and *Look, Stranger!* in 1936. The books were well received, and he earned a reputation as the leading poet of his generation.

Anti-Fascism

Auden loved theater and worked as a playwright throughout the 1930s, producing plays critical of fascism, many in collaboration with his childhood friend Christopher Isherwood. Although gay, he married in 1935, helping his bride Erika Mann, the daughter of novelist Thomas Mann, to escape Nazi Germany. He volunteered as an ambulance driver in Spain during the Spanish Civil War and produced a long, anti-Franco poem about the experience, titled *Spain*, published in 1937. Auden was dismayed by the treatment of priests and Catholic churches in Spain, a hint at his later focus on religious themes in his poetry. During this period, Auden also produced works about travels in Iceland and China. The latter trip formed the basis for his 1939 book, *Journey to War*, written with Isherwood, which addressed in poetry and prose the moral concerns in the years leading up to World War II.

MATURE YEARS

Auden immigrated to the United States with Isherwood in 1939, and naturalized as American in 1946. In the US, he met Chester Kallman, who would become his lifelong companion and occasional collaborator on libretti.

One of Auden's most praised collections, *Another Time*, was published in 1940. It included some of his most famous poems, including "Lullaby" and "September 1, 1939," a political poem Auden grew to hate, denouncing it as dishonest. (After the terrorist attacks on September 11, 2001, the poem was widely shared for its New York setting and its rumination on death and love.) Auden wrote several elegies for the collection, including poems commemorating the poets William Butler Yeats, Matthew Arnold, and A.E. Housman, all of whom had an early influence on his writing.

Return to Christianity

After moving to the United States, Auden re-embraced the Christianity of his youth. The conversion had a profound effect on his later poetry, especially after his Anglican mother's death in 1941. His poetry became increasingly religious after that point, a shift evident in his 1944 collections, *The Sea and the Mirror* and *For the Time Being: A Christmas Oratorio*. Auden even went so far as to revise and reissue many of his earlier poems to reflect his new commitment to Christianity.

In 1947, he published a long dramatic poem, *The Age of Anxiety: A Baroque Eclogue*, about isolation, set in New York during World War II and told from the point of view of four diverse narrators. The poem is heavily alliterative, reminiscent of the Anglo-Saxon poetry he admired in university. It won him the Pulitzer Prize for Poetry in 1948. He published *Nones* in 1951 and *The Shield of Achilles* in 1955, which won the National Book Award for Poetry.

Funeral Blues

W.H. Auden's lyric poem "Stop All the Clocks," sometimes called "Funeral Blues," was recited in its entirety in the funeral scene in the 1994 romantic comedy *Four Weddings and a Funeral*. In the movie, the character Matthew reads the poem as a moving tribute to his late partner, Gareth. Auden first used the poem in a play, *The Ascent of F6*, which he co-authored with Christopher Isherwood in 1936.

Auden's popularity in Britain had waned during World War II, with his emigration to the United States viewed by some as an abandonment, but by the 1950s his reputation had been restored. He returned to Oxford in the prestigious, honorary post of Professor of Poetry from 1956 to 1961, and moved back into his old college in 1972. He lived for a time in Austria and wrote tenderly about his life there with Kallman in *About the House* in 1965.

Wise and Witty

Over the course of his life, Auden was a poet, editor, critic, librettist, and playwright. As a poet, he evolved and wasn't afraid to write in different styles or voices. His work didn't display the experimentation of many Modernists, but even when writing in traditional forms, his voice was still a contemporary voice. Readers turned to him for commentary on current affairs provided from a moral perspective. Like them, Auden was doing his best to try and understand how the world works. More so than almost any other poet of his generation, his poetry was enjoyable to read and hear, filled with a musicality that made even his less-impressive poems sound important.

Auden continued to write and publish collections throughout the later years of his life. One last collection, *Thank You, Fog: Last Poems*, was published after he passed. He died unexpectedly in 1973 while staying at a Viennese hotel.

NATURE POETRY

A Walk in the Woods

Few subjects in poetry have been so revered, so explored, and written about in so many formats as nature. Like peanut butter and chocolate, poetry and nature just go well together. We'll look first at how poems about nature have evolved over the years, then look at a few fine examples.

HISTORY LESSON

The ancient Greeks and Romans wrote about nature, but you won't find Homer or Sappho waxing on about a delightful walk in the woods, although Hesiod did like to write about farming. Nature appears in ancient poems, but it was often described within scenes woven into the larger framework of the poem, or personified in the form of, say, Autumn or Winter. By the third century B.C.E., nature poems took the form of pastorals, written in praise of rural life, when the Greek poet Theocritus wrote his *Idylls*. The Roman poet Virgil also wrote pastorals about shepherds living and working happily in the beautiful countryside. His *Eclogues* and *Georgics* were written around 38 B.C.E.

The anonymous fourteenth-century English poet who wrote *Sir Gawain and the Green Knight* described nature in the changing of the seasons, which in turn, represented the changing phases of life. By the Renaissance, interest in the pastoral had returned. Edmund Spenser's *The Shepheardes Calender* in the sixteenth century was modeled after Virgil's *Eclogues*. Spenser's poem is really twelve poems, one for each month of the year, and includes detailed descriptions not only of the seasons but of the birds and flowers evident at different points in the year. Other lyric poets followed suit, and pastoral poems were written by many of the prominent poets of the day, including Christopher Marlowe and Walter Raleigh.

In the seventeenth century, pastoral poems began to fade in popularity. In Andrew Marvell's "The Garden," published in 1681, he disparages modern society and praises the peace and solitude found in nature, offering a religious perspective on nature's benefits. No shepherds in sight, but it is likely that the garden represents the original biblical Garden of Eden. John Milton's *Paradise Lost* functions similarly, using nature to describe an inner journey. Descriptive landscape poems, sometimes called topographical poems, also gained popularity in this century: John Denham's 1642 poem *Cooper's Hill* was the first of its type. A subgenre was the country house poem, in which poets described in detail the beauty of a patron's rural manor and land, as in Ben Jonson's 1616 poem "To Penshurst."

Many eighteenth-century poems portrayed nature at its best when controlled by man. In James Thomson's *The Seasons*, four blank-verse poems published between 1726 and 1730, he describes natural scenes in great detail, shows a more scientific way of portraying nature, and clearly views its purpose as serving man. Later in the century, William Cowper's poems would show a different attitude, one that celebrates nature for its own sake.

Nature for Healing

For the Romantics, changes in science, technology, and new theological beliefs altered the view of man's central position within nature. They questioned man's sovereignty over the natural world and often attributed a mystical quality to the land. William

Wordsworth wrote about wild nature in a way that helped create the genre of "nature poetry." His poems reflected a belief that time spent outdoors could provide comfort to a troubled soul and a salve for loneliness. His most famous nature poem, "Tintern Abbey," is discussed later in this section.

Haiku

A haiku is a Japanese style of poem that, in English, is written in three unrhymed lines consisting of five, seven, and five syllables. The style is often used for crisp, succinct poems that capture a snapshot of nature. For examples, look for haikus by American poets Richard Wright and Gary Snyder. Writing a haiku based on your own observations of nature can be an excellent exercise to learn how to make every word valuable in a poem.

In the centuries since, we've seen a rich outpouring of nature poetry. As we discussed in earlier sections, American poets Emily Dickinson and Walt Whitman both frequently used nature in their poems, not only to celebrate its beauty but also metaphorically to illustrate inner struggles. Modernist poets, in general, moved away from nature as a topic. Their contemporary, Robert Frost, though, built his reputation on nature poems, writing vividly—and popularly—about his New England landscape. More recently, Beat poet Gary Snyder is known for writing passionately and politically about ecology and the wild. English poet Alice Oswald writes about nature lyrically, but not necessarily romantically. Her heavily researched, book-length poem *Dart*, about the river in Devon, won the 2002 T.S. Eliot Prize, and she has published several collections of nature poems. She is often compared to fellow English nature poet Ted Hughes. The popular Pulitzer Prize–winning American poet Mary Oliver writes beautiful poems about nature as a source of spirituality.

POEMS TO LOVE ABOUT NATURE

Following are some beautiful verses about nature.

"Tintern Abbey" by William Wordsworth

Officially titled "Lines Written a Few Miles above Tintern Abbey, on Revisiting the Banks of the Wye During a Tour, July 13, 1798," this poem was included in *Lyrical Ballads*, the poetry collection Wordsworth published with Samuel Taylor Coleridge in 1798. In "Tintern," Wordsworth introduced his idea that nature could be good for the mind. Composing in blank verse as a monologue, Wordsworth combines concrete imagery and descriptions of the landscape surrounding the abbey with thoughts of how this view, which he had previously seen five years earlier, has changed him for the better. He writes of the power flowing through nature and adopts a worshipful tone of nature itself.

"Stopping by Woods on a Snowy Evening" by Robert Frost

Frost wrote this brief poem in 1922. On the surface, it is simply about a man pausing his sleigh for a few minutes at night in an isolated section of woods before continuing on his way to complete other tasks. Frost composed the four stanzas in an *aaba* rhyme scheme. The simplicity of the poem leaves it open for interpretation. It could be about loneliness, it might be a metaphor for death, or maybe it is a celebration of nature's ability to soothe.

The Leaf and the Cloud by Mary Oliver

Oliver's book-length lyrical poem *The Leaf and the Cloud* was published in 2000. Composed in seven parts, the poem adopts an advisory tone in parts, using concrete images to encourage the reader to get out and experience nature. Like Wordsworth and Frost, Oliver views nature as a restorative place, a way to ease the pains of loneliness, grief, or despair.

ROBERT FROST (1874–1963)

A New England Poet

Robert Frost was one of the most popular, if not *the* most popular, poets of the twentieth century. He was a graceful poet, whose work captured American voices and provided a valuable structured counterpoint to the fragmented poems of many of his peers. Frost received many honors during his life, including four Pulitzer Prizes, awarded in 1924, 1931, 1937, and 1943. He also served as the Consultant in Poetry to the Library of Congress from 1958–1959. His most iconic moment took place at President John F. Kennedy's inauguration in 1961: a grandfatherly, eighty-six-year-old Frost recited from memory his poem, "The Gift Outright," after having to abandon the poem he'd written for the occasion when his notes were impossible to read due to the brightness of the sun.

A FARMER-POET

Frost was born in San Francisco in 1874 to William, a journalist, and Isabelle, a teacher. When he was eleven, after his father's death from tuberculosis, Isabelle moved them back to her home turf, New England. As a child, his mother instilled in him a love of literature, feeding him a steady diet of Shakespeare, Robert Burns, Ralph Waldo Emerson, and William Wordsworth.

In 1895, Frost married Elinor White, his Lawrence, Massachusetts, high school sweetheart and co-valedictorian. As a young man, he briefly attended both Dartmouth and Harvard but did not graduate from either university. He worked as a farmer, and sometimes as a teacher, from 1900 until 1912. He occasionally published poems during this time, but most of his work remained private.

Success in England

It took moving to England in 1912 when he was thirty-eight for his poetry career to launch. His first volume of poems, *A Boy's Will,* was published there in 1913, followed by *North of Boston* in 1914. The latter has stood the test of time better than the former, through poems like "Mending Wall" and "The Death of the Hired Man." While in England, he met Ezra Pound, who wrote glowing reviews of his two books, and he formed close friendships with several other English poets, including Edward Thomas.

A New England Yankee

In 1915, as World War I raged on, he and his family returned to the United States, settling on a farm in Franconia, New Hampshire. By that point, his books had been published in the US, where they were also well received. Frost found work teaching at various colleges while continuing to write poetry. The environment proved conducive to his development as a poet. He found rich material to draw from all around him, cementing not only his reputation as a poet who wrote skillfully about nature but also as one whose ear was tuned to the voice of the people around him. Frost's poetry borrowed from the cadences of his fellow country-dwellers, giving voice to an American—specifically a New England—pattern of speech.

His next publication, a collection of poems called *Mountain Interval,* published in 1916, contained several of his most iconic poems, including "The Road Not Taken," and "Birches." He published four books from 1913 to 1923, accounting for roughly half the poems he would write over his entire lifetime. One of his most well-received books came out in 1942, a collection of short lyrics called *A Witness Tree*. Also in the 1940s, he wrote several popular collections of dramatic poems in blank verse, including *A Masque of Reason* in 1945 and *A Masque of Mercy* in 1947, both of which used biblical themes and characters, and a collection of short lyrics, *Steeple Bush*, in 1947.

FAME BECKONS

Frost became a very famous poet with unusual popularity outside of poetry circles. His verse is accessible, plainspoken but beautiful, and draws from traditional forms. Despite coming of age as a poet during the era of Modernism, his poetry does not reflect the same sensibilities as Ezra Pound, T.S. Eliot, or E.E. Cummings. Rather, he has been compared favorably to writers like William Wordsworth, especially in relation to nature poetry. Frost was adept at executing older poetic forms such as sonnets, pastoral poems, and dramatic monologues. His poems are often playful, even when dealing with serious subjects.

Professor Frost

Robert Frost taught at various institutions throughout his career, primarily for Amherst College, but also as a poet-in-residence everywhere from the University of Michigan to Harvard to Yale. He was one of the founders of the Bread Loaf School of English at Middlebury College. Although he never finished his own degrees, he was granted forty-four honorary ones, including honorary doctorates from Cambridge and Oxford.

Frost was always very concerned with the sound of his poems. He wanted them to appear natural, yet reflect the natural rhythms and meter of real speech. He was a pro at crafting poetry that matched these ideals, a skill that probably helped tremendously in making his poems so popular. He strove, too, for the sound to have meaning, to help push his poems to not simply be pretty but wise. Metaphor is found often in his work and helps to provide it with layers of meaning.

Frost tended to read his lighter poems at public events, but much of his work centers on dark themes, whether lurking beneath the surface or discussed outright. Melancholy and loneliness are often present in his poems; so is outright despair. Frost's carefully cultivated persona obscured his private life, which included periodic bouts of depression. His life was not without its own tragedies: two of his six children died as infants; in 1934, one of his adult daughters died due to complications from childbirth; in 1938, his beloved wife, Elinor, died suddenly; and in 1940, his son committed suicide.

Frost did not fade away as he aged. If anything, his popularity grew. He wrote right up to the end of his long life. In 1962, when he was eighty-eight, he published his last poetry collection, *In the Clearing*. He died of an embolism a year later, on January 29, 1963.

FEMINISM AND POETRY

Equality for All

For centuries, female poets—published female poets, that is—were a rarity. You've learned about a few of them within these pages. All too often, though, writing, *serious* writing, was considered the exclusive domain of men. Even in our modern era, we can count only a few decades where a woman as a poet seems normal, and not a source of surprise or derision. Female poets through the first half of the twentieth century were often the recipient of backhanded praise, praise that either acknowledged their brilliance but viewed it as an anomaly, or praise that claimed the poetry was good, but good for a woman, not *good*.

A poem by a woman doesn't have to be a feminist poem. A poem by a woman is a...poem. And yet, the acknowledgment that poetry is poetry is poetry hasn't come easily. The trailblazers of our previous centuries, who wrote regardless of the conventions of their day, embarked on a path that was later widened—possibly even blown up—by the feminist poets of the 1960s and 1970s. For those decades, a poem by a woman was a political act, a declaration of freedom, a call to join the wider movement for women's equality.

So what now? Feminist poetry is still alive and well. In fact, there was a significant uptick in female empowerment poems that began around January 2017, based on issues that came up during the US presidential election. Slam poetry—performed before an audience—is growing in popularity and often showcases feminist poets who bear witness in verse to the ongoing and imperfect struggle for equality.

But let's circle back now to that idea that a poem by a woman doesn't have to be a feminist poem. Today, women write poems on whatever topic rises forth from their pens and keyboards. And write they do: women write, publish, read, praise, critique, share, and enjoy—in record numbers—poetry.

The Trailblazers

These women writers addressed female equality in their work long before the word *feminism* was either coined or popular. Start with these poems for samples of their subversiveness.

- "No Coward Soul Is Mine" by Emily Brontë
- "After Death" by Christina Rossetti
- "They shut me up in Prose — " by Emily Dickinson
- "I Sit and Sew" by Alice Moore Dunbar-Nelson
- "Helen" by H.D.

THE 1960S AND 1970S

The 1960s and 1970s were periods of great social change in the United States, as well as across Europe. In the US, the civil rights movement, the women's movement, and the gay rights movement all converged to create two decades of unprecedented progress toward equality for oppressed populations. These movements occasionally clashed, but often overlapped, with activists and writers working toward change across race, gender, and sexual lines. The following women represent just a few of the leading feminist poets of these decades. Poets Maya Angelou and Adrienne Rich, who are profiled in their own sections, are among their number.

Audre Lorde (1934–1992)

Black, lesbian, feminist, mother, poet warrior: look up Audre Lorde in any poetry book or online and you will find some combination of these descriptions. Lorde embraced these definitions for herself, believing that women should have the right to define themselves as they see fit. Her poetry passionately, and often fiercely, advocates for female, black, and lesbian autonomy. Start with these: "A Woman Speaks" and "From the House of Yemanjá."

Denise Levertov (1923–1997)

Not all feminist poets choose to be called by that name. Levertov resisted the feminist label but much of her work is clearly feminist in subject and sensibility. More overtly, Levertov is known for her anti-war poetry during the Vietnam War. How women define themselves was a frequent theme for Levertov, which can be seen in her poems "Hypocrite Women," "Looking Glass," and "In Mind."

May Swenson (1913–1989)

Swenson was a highly praised lyric poet whose work was published in more than ten volumes of poetry, beginning in 1954. Her work often centered on themes of love or nature, and often, love of nature. A lesbian writer, she wrote many erotic poems that described sex with creative, unexpected metaphors. She may be best known, however, for *Iconographs*, a collection of concrete poems published in 1970. Concrete poems are written to be viewed, the words forming a shape on the page that illustrates the poem they form. From that collection, "Women" is a poem about sexism shaped in two slender curving columns that evoke the poem's references to pedestals and rocking horses.

Anne Sexton (1928–1974)

Most of Sexton's poems fall into a confessional poet style, a school that emerged in the 1960s with poets who spared their readers no detail on their inner struggles. As a wife and mother, some of Sexton's poems, such as "Housewife," honestly confront the pain she experienced in these roles. Her poems frequently tackled taboo subjects, including adultery and abortion, and her own body, as in the poem "In Celebration of My Uterus." She won the Pulitzer Prize for *Live or Die*, a collection of personal poems about her mental health struggles.

NASTY WOMEN

Although feminist poetry has never really gone away, today it has gained new momentum. Many women are feeling a new urgency about threats to freedoms for women, minorities, and the LGBTQ community and are expressing their views using verse. Poems go viral, circulated online, sometimes providing in almost real-time a response to the day's news. Poet Nina Donovan was just nineteen when actress Ashley Judd read her poem "Nasty Woman" at the Women's March in Washington, DC, in January 2017, prompting a deluge of media attention.

Today's feminist poems reflect the same concerns as their predecessors, but there may be a more concerted effort now for inclusion. Diversity in the form of ethnic and cultural—Hispanic, Asian, Muslim—voices is increasingly being heard, as are those who identify as trans or queer. Bangladeshi-American poet Tarfia Faizullah writes poems about the effects of war on women. Chinese-American Jenny Xie sheds light on the female immigrant experience. Just as earlier generations published women's poems in independent collections to make up for years of silence, it's now possible to find collections such as the 2013 anthology *Troubling the Line: Trans and Genderqueer Poetry and Poetics*.

ADRIENNE RICH (1929–2012)

A Feminist Poet

Few poets are so closely associated with feminism as poet Adrienne Rich. While her ideas are greatly lauded, what makes her stand out is her artistry as a poet. Rich's poems aren't just identity poems or protest poems or lesbian poems. They are precisely composed, eloquent, literary works, with as much care spent on their form and style as on their meaning. Over an evolving, seven-decade career, Rich won almost every prize a poet could win, honored with a MacArthur Fellowship, a National Book Award, the Ruth Lilly Poetry Prize, the National Book Critics Circle Award, the Wallace Stevens Award, and, later in life, the National Book Foundation's Medal for Distinguished Contribution to American Letters. She famously refused the 1997 National Medal of Arts, the highest honor the US government grants artists, to protest racial and economic injustices.

HOUSEWIFE TO ACTIVIST

Rich was born in Baltimore, Maryland, on May 16, 1929, the daughter of a prominent Jewish doctor and a Christian musician mother. Her parents were intellectuals, and Rich was pushed from childhood to achieve academically, even writing poems under her father's strict, demanding eye. As a student at Radcliffe, Rich later noted that her education included no female professors and no female poets. Her poetry career got off to an impressive start when poet W.H. Auden chose her first book, *A Change of World*, for the prestigious Yale

Younger Poets Prize in 1951. Her early work was praised for its technical prowess and skillful use of meter and rhyme.

Rich was a dynamic poet whose work, and life, passed through many phases. She married young, in 1953, to Alfred Conrad, an economics professor at Harvard. She became a mother soon after, raising three boys. Rich strained against the expectations placed on her as a woman, constraints that were nonexistent for her male poet peers. Her domestic experience—the responsibilities of cooking, cleaning, and mothering—would have a profound effect on her later poetry and efforts as an activist. In her 1963 collection, *Snapshots of a Daughter-in-Law*, Rich eviscerates traditional marriages.

Writing with Intensity

Rich was active in the civil rights, women's, and antiwar movements. She and Conrad moved to New York in 1966, where they joined Vietnam-resistance groups and Rich taught poetry to disadvantaged students. Her work began a major shift during this period. She adopted a less formal style and infused her writing with more intensity, passion, and emotion. She began the practice of including the date with her poems, as if by pinning the sentiments expressed to a specific time she'd be free to change her mind later. The poems in this new style were collected and published in *Leaflets* in 1969 and *The Will to Change* in 1971. The books resonated with female readers and launched Rich into her public persona as a feminist. Her marriage broke up in 1970. Not long after, Conrad committed suicide.

Her next book of poetry, *Diving into the Wreck,* published in 1973, was a popular and critical success. The title poem is considered one of the greatest poems to emerge from the women's movement. She won the National Book Award for the collection, which she chose to accept in the name of all women with fellow feminist nominees Alice

Walker and Audre Lorde. Her later work, *The Dream of a Common Language*, in 1978, continued the exploration of feminist themes and rebellion against the male-dominated culture.

A VERSATILE POET

Throughout her career, Rich experimented with using different forms of poetry. In the late 1960s, she wrote several ghazals, an Arabic form. "The Blue Ghazals (9/21/68)" and "Ghazals: Homage to Ghalib" honor nineteenth-century ghazals written in Urdu. Rich deviated from the usual style by choosing not to use rhyme. She riffed off of the sonnet form for a collection of lesbian love poems, *Twenty-One Love Poems*, published in 1976. The volume also served as Rich's public coming out as a lesbian; she and fellow writer Michelle Cliff were companions for more than thirty years. Rich turned to long-form poetry for her 1991 book, *An Atlas of the Difficult World*, composed in thirteen sections. Like Walt Whitman, Rich sought to create a poem that documented and explored her love of country.

Ghazals

The term *ghazal* means "talk about love" in Arabic. A ghazal is a Middle Eastern lyric poem comprising between five and fifteen couplets, which dates to seventh-century Arabia. Each couplet is independent from every other couplet but is connected by a limited rhyme scheme. The first couplet rhymes and subsequent couplets use that rhyme in the second line. (Often, the same word is used.) Another convention is to include the poet's name in the last couplet. Traditionally, ghazals are sung.

Rich's poetic output continued throughout her life. Her later works include *Telephone Ringing in the Labyrinth* in 2007 and *Tonight No Poetry Will Serve* in 2011.

Rich also wrote essays and nonfiction. She published *Of Woman Born: Motherhood as Experience and Institution,* one of the first scholarly works to examine motherhood, in 1976. Her career included teaching at universities, including City College of New York, Columbia, Swarthmore, Bryn Mawr, and Stanford University. Rich and Cliff edited *Sinister Wisdom,* a lesbian literary journal, for several years.

A tireless activist, Rich was the first to admit that poetry alone does not create change. As she said in 2006 when she received her National Book Foundation medal, "Poetry is not a healing lotion, an emotional massage, a kind of linguistic aromatherapy." But Rich's body of work shed light on the unique experiences of women—sometimes specifically Jewish, lesbian women—an illumination that helped to show their humanity and worth, and their intrinsic right to an equal life.

She died in 2012 at her home in Santa Cruz, California.

MAYA ANGELOU (1928–2014)

Poet, Performer, Activist

Maya Angelou is an artist whose life defied expectations at every turn. Angelou overcame the odds of growing up poor, black, and female in a pre-civil rights America to become a literary powerhouse whose output included thirty-six books, including seven of poetry and six autobiographies.

A FULL LIFE

Marguerite Annie Johnson was born in St. Louis, Missouri, in 1928, to Bailey Johnson, a navy cook, and Vivian Baxter, an occasional nightclub singer. Angelou had an itinerant childhood, living first in California, then shuttling between the small town of Stamps, Arkansas, and St. Louis before landing in Oakland, California, for her high school years.

Angelou's parents divorced when she was little, prompting her father to send her and her brother, Bailey, to live with his mother in Stamps, Arkansas. Annie "Momma" Henderson ran the general store for Stamps's tight-knit black community. At one point, Angelou was sent to live with her mother's family in St. Louis, with tragic consequences. As an eight-year-old, she was raped by an older man, and subsequently stopped speaking for several years. She later returned to Arkansas to live with Momma Henderson. As a teen, she moved again, this time to California. Shortly after finishing high school, at seventeen, she gave birth to her son, Guy Johnson.

Angelou is not a writer who forged a straight path into the publishing world. As a young woman, she held various working-class jobs, including a stint in San Francisco as a streetcar conductor, as well as, briefly, a prostitute. Later, as an actress and dancer, she toured Europe in a production of *Porgy and Bess*, performed on and off Broadway, and was nominated for a Tony Award; she studied with modern dance icon Martha Graham; and she was nominated for an Emmy Award for a role in the televised 1970s miniseries *Roots*. She was also able to be a newspaper editor in Cairo, Egypt, and Accra, Ghana; a university administrator in Ghana; and, after establishing her writing career, a professor at Wake Forest University.

Angelou was active in the civil rights movement of the 1950s and 1960s. She worked for both Malcom X, helping to build his Organization of Afro-American Unity, and Martin Luther King Jr., as the northern coordinator for King's Southern Christian Leadership Conference.

She married twice: Tosh Angelos, from 1951 to 1954, and Paul du Feu, from 1974 to 1983.

ANGELOU THE WRITER

Now that we've established she lived a fascinating life, let's talk about her writing. Angelou was a poet, an essayist, a playwright, a screenwriter, and an editor. In the early 1950s, Angelou joined the Harlem Writers Guild. At the time, she was working as a professional actress and dancer. It wasn't until the late 1960s that she turned seriously to writing. At the urging of novelist James Baldwin, Angelou began work on an autobiography.

When *I Know Why the Caged Bird Sings* was published in 1969, it made an immediate splash. It was a new kind of memoir, innovative for its time and nonlinear, and used many fiction techniques to tell the story of Angelou's childhood and teens. Her candid portrayals of racism and sexual violence attracted both controversy and praise. The book was nominated for a National Book Award and launched Angelou's career as a writer. Over the next thirty years, she would write five more memoirs, chronicling different stages in her life, culminating in 2002's *A Song Flung Up to Heaven* covering the tumultuous civil rights years of 1964 to 1968.

After the success of *I Know Why the Caged Bird Sings,* Angelou took up poetry. Her 1971 poetry collection, *Just Give Me a Cool Drink of Water 'fore I Diiie,* was nominated for a Pulitzer Prize. She usually wrote in free verse with a flowing rhythm and cadence that begged to be read out loud. Just as she had with her nonfiction, Angelou looked unflinchingly at racial and political concerns. Her poems are unapologetically feminist and honest about her personal struggles as a black woman. There's a strong thread of hope in her poetry too. Despite her early struggles in life, she held strongly to a belief in a shared humanity.

Her subsequent collections include *Oh Pray My Wings Are Gonna Fit Me Well* in 1975; *Shaker, Why Don't You Sing?* in 1983; *I Shall Not Be Moved* in 1990; *Wouldn't Take Nothing for My Journey Now* in 1993; *The Complete Collected Poems of Maya Angelou* in 1994; and *A Brave and Startling Truth* in 1995.

Honors and Accolades

Of all her honors, the most visible one was given to her by President Bill Clinton, who asked Angelou to deliver his Inauguration Day poem. Angelou was only the second poet in history—the first was Robert Frost—to be so honored. On January 20, 1993, Angelou welcomed the new president with an original poem, "On the Pulse of Morning," which celebrated the commonality of humankind and struck a hopeful and optimistic tone for social justice for all. Its cadences and message were reminiscent of Martin Luther King Jr.'s "I Have a Dream" speech.

Angelou was a presidential guest again in 2005, when she delivered the poem "Amazing Peace" for President George W. Bush at the White House tree-lighting ceremony. She addressed a climate of "fear and apprehension" but assured her listeners with stirring language that peace was coming.

In 2000, President Clinton awarded her the National Medal of Arts. In 2010, President Barack Obama gave her the Presidential Medal of Freedom, the highest civilian honor in the United States. More than fifty universities gave her honorary degrees. Presidents Ford and Carter both asked her to serve on presidential committees.

Angelou stayed active as a speaker, writer, and activist almost until the day she died. She passed away at her home in Winston-Salem, North Carolina, on May 28, 2014.

Grammy Award Winner

Maya Angelou was nominated five times for a Grammy Award. She won three times in the Best Spoken Word category: in 1993 for her audio recording of the inaugural poem "On the Pulse of Morning"; in 1995 for her recording of the poem "Phenomenal Woman"; and in 2002 for her recording of *A Song Flung Up to Heaven*.

AFRICAN-AMERICAN POETS

Finding Their Voice

African-American poetry had to struggle for a share of the literary landscape in America. African-American poets have moved from barely acknowledging their experience of race to advocating for equality to embracing an independent literary tradition that sits both beside, and firmly within, the wider American poetic culture.

PRE–HARLEM RENAISSANCE

Phillis Wheatley, a young slave in Massachusetts, wrote the first published book of African-American poetry. *Poems on Various Subjects, Religious and Moral*, printed in London in 1773, contained thirty-eight poems, as well as a woodcut image of Wheatley writing at a desk, a letter from her master, and a letter authenticating Wheatley as the true author of the poems and signed by members of Boston's elite.

In 1829, the slave George Moses Horton wrote about slavery in his collection *The Hope of Liberty* but failed to sell enough copies to earn his own freedom. Abolitionist and orator Frances Ellen Watkins Harper, who had been born free in Maryland in 1825, had considerably more success writing on slavery with her 1854 collection *Poems on Miscellaneous Subjects*. The book went through twenty editions in the next twenty years.

In 1893, Paul Laurence Dunbar published *Oak and Ivy*, establishing him as one of America's best lyric poets. Dunbar wrote many poems using a dialect instead of standard English, and to his regret, those were the poems that gave him fame and accolades. We'll explore his work, which achieved bestseller status in his lifetime, more in another section.

HARLEM RENAISSANCE

The Harlem Renaissance began in Harlem in the 1920s and lasted until the early 1930s. The period is often associated with the ascent of jazz and blues within musical traditions, but poetry was also a vital part of the movement's creative output. Poets of the time celebrated black culture and the freedom to express themselves. While African-American poets of earlier generations had avoided writing about race, the subject moved to the front and center for Harlem Renaissance writers. Poet Claude McKay gave voice to the anger and frustration that many blacks felt living in a racist society with his 1922 publication of *Harlem Shadows*. Poet Jean Toomer celebrated his African-American identity in *Cane*, an experimental collection of poetry and prose published in 1923. Toomer's poems covered the experiences of blacks farming in the South as well as those living in the urban North and did so with a lyrical, expressive, and philosophical style that earned him may accolades.

Countee Cullen was one of the movement's most prominent poets. A graduate of New York University who went on to get a master's degree from Harvard, Cullen's first book of lyric poetry, *Color*, established him in 1925 as the most famous black writer of his time, popular in both white and black literary circles. *Color* included many poems on African-American themes, written using sonnet or ballad forms, and addressed in stark terms the difficulties of being black. He wrote two more volumes of poetry, *Copper Sun* in 1927, and *The*

Ballad of the Brown Girl in 1927. Cullen received numerous literary prizes and was later awarded a Guggenheim Fellowship.

Women of the Harlem Renaissance

Although their reputations were eclipsed by the men, women were also an important part of the movement. Angelina Weld Grimké wrote brief Imagist poems; Alice Moore Dunbar-Nelson wrote traditional poems about romance with a modern sensibility; Anne Spencer was a feminist poet whose work ranged from Romantic to Modernist traditions; and Georgia Douglas Johnson wrote love poems, published four volumes of poetry, and regularly hosted Harlem Renaissance poets in her Washington, DC, home.

Langston Hughes, like many other poets of the movement, turned to black folklore, spirituals, and myths for inspiration. He is widely considered the poet laureate of Harlem. Sterling A. Brown was also a folk poet who experimented with black musical forms in his work. Brown's first volume of poetry, *Southern Road*, was published in 1932 and showcased his skill at transforming folk speech into vivid, emotional poetry. For example, his four-part poem "Ma Rainey" sizzles and pops on the page, conveying not only the magic of a Ma Rainey performance but the profound effect that her singing had on her audiences.

Cullen and Hughes publicly debated what it meant to be a black poet. Cullen rejected the idea that he was a black poet and not simply a poet, and Hughes argued that being black was an integral part of their identities as poets. Cullen was criticized for not writing more about race, especially in his second book.

TWENTIETH CENTURY AND BEYOND

In the 1940s and 1950s, many new poets emerged. In 1942, Margaret Walker won the Yale Younger Poets Prize for her book of ballads, sonnets, and free verse, *For My People*. Melvin Tolson's finest work was his avant-garde collection *Harlem Gallery*, published in 1965, which reviewers compared favorably to Walt Whitman and T.S. Eliot. Robert Hayden wrote brilliant Modernist poems on historical African-American subjects.

In 1950, Gwendolyn Brooks was the first African American to receive the Pulitzer Prize, winning for *Annie Allen*. Brooks was a poet who could write skillfully and beautifully in almost any form, as adept at sonnets as free verse and ballads. She wrote passionately about the African-American community, especially about her fellow Chicagoans. She was the Consultant in Poetry to the Library of Congress from 1985–1986 and the poet laureate for Illinois from 1968–2000.

Black Arts Movement

The US civil rights movement, which began in the 1950s with the desegregation of public schools, was in full swing in the 1960s. The desire for equality, and often, a separate African-American literature and community, motivated many of that era's black poets. Poet and playwright Amiri Baraka and theater scholar and poet Larry Neal edited *Black Fire*, the pivotal anthology of the Black Arts movement with poetry, fiction, essays, and plays. Brooks was a participant in the movement, which inspired her to write poetry directly addressing racism. Nikki Giovanni wrote from a militant African-American perspective in her collections *Black Feeling, Black Talk* in 1967 and *Black Judgement* in 1968.

1970s to Present

Nikki Giovanni, Lucille Clifton, Sonia Sanchez, Audre Lorde, and Jay Wright began their careers during the Black Arts movement but continued to write and publish for decades after, evolving in style and subject matter. Although poets continue to address race and racism, there is more freedom now to write about any subject.

In recent decades, African-American poets have garnered some of the world's highest accolades. The young African-American poet Tracy K. Smith was appointed US poet laureate in 2017 and had previously won the Pulitzer Prize in 2012 for her collection *Life on Mars*. She follows in the footsteps of Natasha Trethewey, who served as poet laureate from 2012 to 2014 and won the Pulitzer in 2007 for *Native Guard*. Rita Dove served as US poet laureate from 1993 to 1995 and won the Pulitzer in 1987 for *Thomas and Beulah*. Other Pulitzer Prize winners include Tyehimba Jess for *Olio* in 2017 and Yusef Komunyakaa for *Neon Vernacular: New and Selected Poems* in 1994. Derek Walcott won the Nobel Prize in Literature in 1992 for his body of work.

LANGSTON HUGHES (1902–1967)

I, Too, Sing America

As a leading member of the Harlem Renaissance, Langston Hughes helped usher in a new era of African-American poetry. Hughes focused on writing poetry unique to the experiences of black Americans. Hughes wrote more than 860 poems during his lifetime, exploring many aspects of black culture. His writing career, which included poetry, drama, fiction, and essays, stretched from the 1920s until his death in the late 1960s.

YOUNG, BLACK, AND TALENTED

Hughes's grandmother, Mary Langston, instilled in him a sense of pride about his heritage. Mary Langston had been married twice: first to a man who had died at Harper's Ferry fighting alongside John Brown and then to Hughes's grandfather, a strident abolitionist.

Hughes was born in Joplin, Missouri, to James and Carrie Hughes. Shortly after his birth, his parents separated and James moved to Mexico. Hughes moved around during his childhood, but spent most of it in Lawrence, Kansas, before moving to Cleveland in 1916. While attending Central High School, he started writing poetry for the school's literary journal.

After spending a year in Mexico with his father, Hughes enrolled in 1921 in Columbia University in New York. That year, he published his first poem, "The Negro Speaks of Rivers," published in *Crisis* magazine, edited by NAACP co-founder W.E.B. Du Bois. When his funds ran out after a year, Hughes dropped out of Columbia, taking on menial jobs around the world for several years. He worked as a dishwasher in Paris and served meals on ships to both Europe and Africa. His travels also took him to the Azores and the Canary Islands.

He returned to Harlem for several years, writing poems, and lived in Washington, DC, before earning a scholarship to attend the historically black Lincoln University in Pennsylvania in 1926. He graduated in 1929.

The Folk Poet

Hughes published his first volume of poetry, *The Weary Blues*, in 1926, followed by *Fine Clothes to the Jew* in 1927. Hughes had grown up surrounded by the working poor. When he set pen to paper, their stories and struggles are what inspired him. That didn't sit well with some members of the African-American establishment, who argued that blacks needed to put only their best image forward and that showing themselves in a negative light only reinforced racists' opinions of them. Hughes pushed back. He agreed there was a need to raise the image of blacks but that there was room for honest portrayals of lives like the ones he knew, people who were good people, even if they were poor.

Hughes was a versatile poet who often experimented with forms and language. His style and subject matter—regular Americans—have drawn comparisons to free-verse poets Walt Whitman and Carl Sandburg. Hughes was inspired by their work. One of his most famous poems, "I, Too," is a response to Walt Whitman's nineteenth-century poem "I Hear America Singing." In Hughes's version, the speaker addresses his desire for a place at the table, and belief that he'll get one soon.

African-American musical forms—including the blues and jazz, field and work songs, and ballads—were a source of inspiration for Hughes. His efforts to combine the forms with poetry earned him both praise and insults. Some found his work to be too derivative and simple while others believed he was creating a new, uniquely black art form. His embrace of the rhythms of blues and jazz is evident in poems like "Jazzonia" and "To a Black Dancer in 'The Little Savoy.'"

The Blues and Langston Hughes

The roots of the blues are found in the songs slaves sung while working in the fields of the American South. Although the term *blues* can be used to describe a sad song, it can also refer to a more formal version of a three-line song comprising two nearly identical lines followed by a rhyming third line. Hughes was one of the first poets to adopt the style to his poetry. He chose to combine the three lines into six-line stanzas, with rhymes in the second, fourth, and sixth lines.

Hughes also used humor in his poems. In his blues-riffed poem "Morning After" he jokes about the "little bit o' woman" who sounds like a "great big crowd" when she snores. The humor helped make his poetry accessible to the public, even if it meant some critics accused Hughes of being unintellectual in his approach to race.

TAKING MORAL MEASURE

Hughes refused to accept the status quo of America as a racist nation and spent the forty years of his writing career working to challenge that racism. Poetry was just one of his creative outlets; he also wrote novels and short-story collections; essays; two memoirs; books on black history; plays and musicals for Broadway; a screenplay; and he translated books. He worked as a war correspondent in Spain during the 1930s. For more than twenty years, beginning in 1943, he penned a syndicated newspaper column, later collected in books, based on a fictional character, Jessie B. Semple, nicknamed "Simple." Simple was a poor Harlem man whose experiences were relatable to blacks across the country.

Hughes's later poetic volumes include *Montage of a Dream Deferred* in 1951, *Ask Your Mama* in 1961, and *The Panther and the Lash* in 1967. In the 1960s, Hughes fell out of popularity among some black writers. The civil rights movement brought with it a new, more militant, style of black poetry. Hughes's belief in the inherent good of all mankind wasn't welcome in the Black Arts movement, whose poets had grown frustrated with waiting patiently for whites to show their better natures. Hughes's poetry, especially in *The Panther and the Lash*, was out of step with the politically charged poems of the day. Black poets wanted him to do more than take a moral stand; they wanted a political one too.

Hughes died of cancer on May 22, 1967, in New York City. Since his death, his work has continued to be published, including two volumes of poetry for children: 1994's *The Sweet and Sour Animal Book,* illustrated with drawings by kids at the Harlem School of the Arts, and 1995's *The Block*, illustrated with collages by artist Romare Bearden. Hughes's poetry continues to be read and appreciated by new generations and his place is firmly acknowledged within the canon of African-American literature.

PAUL LAURENCE DUNBAR (1872–1906)

The Caged Bird Sings

Shortly before the advent of the twentieth century, Paul Laurence Dunbar was the first black poet to find a national audience. During his short life, Dunbar established a literary reputation for himself at a time when it was extremely difficult for African Americans to be published, let alone share their work with a wide audience. Some of his poetry can be controversial: Dunbar sometimes used a dialect instead of standard English in his poems.

THE STRUGGLE FOR ACCEPTANCE

Dunbar was born on June 27, 1872, in Dayton, Ohio, to parents who were former slaves in Kentucky. His father, Joshua Dunbar, had escaped slavery and served in the Civil War. His mother, Matilda Murphy, taught him how to read. Both parents shared with Dunbar stories that had been passed down to them.

Dunbar was the only black student at Dayton's Central High School, where he distinguished himself as an excellent student. He edited the school newspaper, was president of the literary society, and wrote the class song's lyrics.

After high school, Dunbar's talent wasn't enough to overcome racial prejudice when he tried to find employment as a writer. Instead, he worked as an elevator operator at a Dayton hotel. He continued to write poetry, as well as fiction and essays, during breaks at work and whenever he could find the time. In 1892, at the invitation of one of his former teachers, Dunbar was asked to read his poems at the Western Association of Writers when they held their annual meeting in Dayton. The event helped him to make several useful introductions.

Friendship with Orville Wright

Aviation pioneer Orville Wright was one of Dunbar's twenty-eight classmates at Central High in Dayton. The two were good friends. Dunbar and Wright collaborated for a year to publish Dayton's first African-American newspaper, the *Dayton Tattler*, edited by Dunbar and printed by Wright's printing business. Wright also printed ads and tickets for Dunbar's early poetry readings.

By 1893, he had enough poems to self-publish a collection, *Oak and Ivy*. Orville Wright's print shop didn't have the ability to bind books, but Wright's father Milton was a deacon at the United Brethren Church, which operated a publishing house with the right equipment. To recoup costs, Dunbar supposedly sold copies to guests of the hotel who rode in his elevator.

GROWING REPUTATION

Slowly, Dunbar's poems circulated into literary circles. He found supporters and benefactors—including abolitionist Frederick Douglass—who helped fund his second collection, *Majors and Minors*, in 1895. William Dean Howells, a highly influential critic and novelist, wrote a glowing review of the book in *Harper's Weekly*, a major literary magazine of the time. Howells helped arrange for Dunbar's third book,

Lyrics of Lowly Life, to be professionally published in 1896. The book, which consisted mainly of poems from his first two collections, was a bestseller and turned Dunbar into a household name.

Essentially, there were two styles of poems included in *Lyrics of Lowly Life*. As a student, Dunbar had absorbed the work of the Romantic poets, including John Keats, William Wordsworth, and Samuel Taylor Coleridge, as well as Scottish poet Robert Burns. Their influence is evident in poems such as "Sympathy," which eloquently described the stress and pain of a caged bird that longs to be free. (Poet Maya Angelou borrowed Dunbar's last line, "I know why the caged bird sings," for the title of her 1969 autobiography.) The standard English poems are beautifully written and show a maturity in style.

The second style of poems included were dialect poems, written to sound like the speech of African-American Southerners. Howells signaled these out as exemplary in an introduction to *Lyrics of Lowly Life*, and those poems were the ones that proved most popular with white readers. The dialect poems were well written but their success, to Dunbar's chagrin, overshadowed the brilliance of his other poems.

Confronting Stereotypes

The dialect poems are problematic for Dunbar's reputation. They were a common style of poetry in the 1890s, usually written by whites. Dialect poems helped to popularize stereotypes of plantation life, provided unflattering caricatures of blacks, and sanitized the violent realities of racism. As a black writer, Dunbar would have faced a lot of pressure to conform to the era's conventions and compose poems that would gain him a wider audience. Nearly all African-American poets published in the ten years after *Lyrics* came out also published dialect poems.

As scholars have reexamined his work in the context of his times, his reputation is recovering. Some find evidence of protest within some of his poems, including "We Wear the Mask," which refers to a tortured soul underneath a "mask that grins and lies." In "The Poet," Dunbar's speaker laments a poet's efforts to sing a "deeper note," when the world acclaims only a "jingle in a broken tongue."

PROLIFIC FINAL DECADE

In 1897, Dunbar traveled to England for six months to promote his work and found a British publisher for *Lyrics of a Lowly Life*. From 1897 to 1902, Dunbar lived in Washington, DC, where he worked as a clerk at the Library of Congress. In 1898, he married poet Alice Moore, who joined him in DC. The marriage was short-lived: they separated in 1902. By that point, Dunbar was battling tuberculosis and depression and self-medicating with alcohol.

Despite his personal and physical difficulties, Dunbar was incredibly prolific during the last few years of his life. He broke another barrier as the first African American to publish a short-story collection when *Folks from Dixie* appeared and was well received in 1898. He went on to publish three additional books of short stories. He published three unsuccessful novels and one reasonably success-ful one, *The Sport of the Gods*. Additional poetry collections included *Lyrics of the Hearthside* and *Lyrics of Love and Laughter*. Two more collections compiled previously published poems.

He returned to Dayton to the home he had purchased for his mother before his death of tuberculosis at thirty-three. Like other talented poets who died too soon, it's impossible to say what he might have achieved if he'd had more time. His legacy, however, lives on in the many cul-tural barriers his success helped break, paving the way for the entry of African-American poets writing during the Harlem Renaissance.

CONTEMPORARY MOVEMENTS

Seeking the New

Every historical period has brought with it new approaches to poetry: the twentieth century is no exception. Poetry written since the end of World War II is broadly referred to as contemporary poetry. It encompasses a wide variety of styles, everything from post-Modern works that shatter previously held conceptions of poetry to poems that adhere closely to traditional forms.

CONTEMPORARY CHARACTERISTICS

Let's look at a few of the common characteristics that serve to differentiate contemporary poetry from earlier eras, recognizing these are generalities referring to overall trends.

Intimate and Personal

Especially in contrast to their immediate predecessors, the Modernists, contemporary poets are willing to insert themselves into their poetry. Poets share their individual personalities and don't shy away from intimate, personal details about themselves. Contemporary poems are more likely to be written in the first person than in other eras, with "I" appearing frequently. Rather than adopt a persona, the voice of the speaker in the poem is more commonly the voice of the poet. Sylvia Plath writes about her attempts at suicide in "Lady Lazarus" and Allen Ginsberg shares about his time in a mental hospital in "Howl." The emphasis on the personal also means contemporary poems are less overtly intellectual; they tend not to be burdened with numerous, obscure external references such as in a poem like T.S. Eliot's *The Waste Land*.

Sexual Honesty

Poets writing about sex isn't necessarily a radical notion—sex was a topic even for Roman and Greek poets. But sexual frankness, especially regarding homosexuality, was largely absent from mainstream poetry for centuries. Contemporary poets as a group have produced a large body of poems that address sexuality without embarrassment. They don't hide behind metaphor or symbolism or ambiguous pronouns. Adrienne Rich wrote openly about being a lesbian and Robert Duncan about being gay.

Irony and Wit

Irony—the difference between reality and appearance—is frequently present in contemporary poems. Irony adds complexity to a poem by having it function on two levels, lending power to the poet's true meaning, which sits below the surface. Some contemporary poets, like Frank O'Hara, use it to comic effect, as in his poem "Poem [Lana Turner has collapsed!]." Billy Collins also frequently uses irony, sometimes to deflate the pretentiousness of the poetry world, seen in his poems "Introduction to Poetry" and "Workshop." Poet Lucille Clifton used dark humor to shed light on the African-American female experience, a quality present in her poems "here rests" and "Admonitions."

Diversity

Contemporary poetry encompasses the work of poets from a wide variety of backgrounds. Change comes slowly, but since the 1950s, poetry by people of color, including African Americans, Latinos,

Asians, and Native Americans, has grown steadily in popularity, existing not only as niche poetry—produced within and for a particular population—but as part of the mainstream.

Everyday Language

"Thee" and "thou" are out; "Yo" and "LOL" are in. Contemporary poetry is generally written in contemporary language. Following on from Walt Whitman and William Carlos Williams, who envisioned an American poetic language, today's poets tend to write as people speak. Slang and obscenities, natural patterns of speech, and vocabulary that doesn't require a dictionary are employed to create poems that address readers as we would our own peers.

Free Verse versus Traditional Forms

Here is where we stumble when trying to characterize contemporary poems. Some contemporary poets revel in creating work that defies definition or turns traditional forms on their head. John Berryman won a Pulitzer in 1965 for *77 Dream Songs* and a National Book Award in 1969 for *His Toy, His Dream, His Rest*, using an invented style and form that drew from both slang and Shakespeare. C.K. Williams's 1977 *With Ignorance* had to be specially printed in a wide-page format to accommodate the poetry's extremely long lines. Many poets, though, including Robert Lowell, Donald Justice, W.S. Merwin, and John Ashbery, have produced celebrated work both within and beyond traditional forms. Ashbery's *The Tennis Court Oath* is stylistically radical, but he also writes in traditional forms such as the sestina and pantoum.

CONTEMPORARY SCHOOLS

Classifying poets into schools is useful to a point. It helps critics and readers to identify trends in poetry and to view the work of poets in relation to one another. However, most poets write across movements, with poems that can't quite be classified as either one thing or another. Below are a few of the more prominent contemporary movements.

Black Mountain Poets

This movement, sometimes referred to as projective verse, formed at Black Mountain College in North Carolina and existed from 1933 to 1956. Black Mountain poets sought to widen poetry out from the individual to bigger examinations of human identity. They sought to write "open" verse, which emphasized thought and emotion as well as using breath to create natural line lengths. Charles Olson, Robert Creeley, and Robert Duncan were prominent members, with Denise Levertov and Paul Carroll loosely affiliated.

New York School

This school refers to experimental poets living in New York City in the early 1950s. Many of the poets were also closely associated with the city's abstract expressionist painters. Characterizing their work is difficult—the poets were all highly individualistic—but in general, they sought to write avant-garde poetry that pushed boundaries for the day. Members included Barbara Guest, John Ashbery, and Frank O'Hara.

San Francisco Renaissance

Associated with the Beats, the San Francisco Renaissance occurred between 1955 and 1965. Participants emphasized the individual's role in poetry and eliminated restrictions on how poetry could be constructed. Performing poems publicly was intrinsic to their philosophy. Prominent poets include Kenneth Rexroth, Philip Whalen, and Gary Snyder.

Language Poets

Language poets refers to experimental poets who became prominent in the late 1970s and 1980s. These poets viewed poetry as a theoretical exercise. They subverted and dissected grammar, syntax, and narrative as a way of critiquing or upending society. Aggressively post-Modern, their work takes shape in barely recognizable, hard-to-interpret, creative forms.

Speculative Poetry

By no means a major contemporary movement, speculative poetry has a dedicated fan base. Speculative poetry has a wide definition, but it encompasses science fiction, horror, mythology, and fantasy. Consider it *Game of Thrones* for poetry, with speculative poets seeking to answer the question "What if?"

SYLVIA PLATH (1932–1963)

A Confessional Poet

Sylvia Plath was a talented American poet whose life ended tragically by suicide when she was thirty. Plath is closely associated with her English husband, the poet Ted Hughes. A confessional poet, Plath's deeply personal, often anguished, sometimes violent poems were written with great technical skill and continue to resonate deeply with readers.

AMBITIOUS PATH

Plath was born in 1932 in Boston, Massachusetts, to Otto and Aurelia Plath. Otto was a German immigrant who taught German and entomology at Boston University. He and Aurelia had met when she was his student. When Plath was eight, Otto died after his foot was amputated due to untreated diabetes. Plath's grief would fester and become fodder for later poems.

Plath was precocious and a good student and writer. The summer before her freshman year of college, a short story she wrote was published in *Seventeen* magazine. She attended Smith College on a full scholarship and while there, won prizes for her poetry and writing. Plath struggled with depression, though, and suffered a breakdown while on a school break. She received shock treatments, attempted suicide, and was hospitalized. When she returned to college, she continued to excel academically. She graduated in 1955 and won a Fulbright Fellowship to pursue a graduate degree in English at Cambridge University's Newnham College.

THE CAMBRIDGE YEARS

During her first year at Cambridge, Plath met a young man at a literary magazine launch. Ted Hughes was a recent graduate who also was an aspiring poet. The attraction was immediate. Four months later, in June 1956, they were married. Both poets had written books and were seeking publication. Hughes was the first to find a publisher, for *The Hawk in the Rain* in 1957, after winning a contest in which Plath had entered him. (She had typed the poems and mailed them in for him.) *The Hawk in the Rain* launched Hughes's writing career.

The Boston Years

Soon after, in 1957, Hughes and Plath accepted teaching positions in the United States: Plath at Smith and Hughes at the University of Massachusetts. The academic life didn't work out—Plath found teaching distracting from writing—so after a year the couple moved on to Boston. Plath worked secretarial jobs part time and enrolled in a writing class taught by poet Robert Lowell. One of her classmates was Anne Sexton. Plath was competitive professionally with Sexton, although they were close friends.

Confessional Poetry

Both Sylvia Plath and Anne Sexton wrote in a confessional style, which meant sharing intimate thoughts and feelings. Their instructor, Robert Lowell, was one of the first poets to adopt the style, which developed during the 1950s and 1960s. Confessional poets broke taboos by writing about subjects like depression and grief with brutal honesty. Although the emotions portrayed in the poems were raw, the poems themselves were polished and carefully constructed.

FINAL YEARS

Plath and Hughes moved back to England in December 1959. The next year, Plath gave birth to their daughter, Frieda. Plath's dream of publishing also came true that year: published in London, her collection of poems, *The Colossus*, was greeted with critical praise. Reviewers found in her work favorable echoes of W.H. Auden and William Butler Yeats.

In the summer of 1961, the family moved to rural Devon. Plath continued to write, often at a frenetic pace, rising early to push poems out before breakfast. She wrote whenever she had time during the day, between household tasks. She suffered a miscarriage at one point and had an appendectomy. She became pregnant again and gave birth to Nicholas in January 1962.

That year was a difficult one for Plath. She and Hughes separated after she learned that he had been carrying on an affair. She packed the children up and moved to a tiny apartment in London. She dealt with her pain by furiously writing. In under a year, she produced enough poems to fill three subsequent collections. The poems probably reflect her state of mind. Bitter with staccato rhythms, they reveal a creative mind who was no longer concerned with adhering to norms. In them, Plath lashes out harshly against domesticity and marriage.

On February 11, 1963, at age thirty, Plath took her own life. In the middle of the night, she put out milk and bread for her toddler's and baby's breakfast and stuck her head in the gas oven.

LEGACY

While living in Devon, Plath had written a radio play called *Three Women*, warmly celebrating the friendships women formed on a maternity ward, which the BBC produced and aired in 1962. She also published short stories and one novel, the autobiographical *The Bell Jar*, originally published under the pseudonym Victoria Lucas, shortly before she died.

Prior to her death, Plath had been preparing a manuscript for her second poetry collection. Hughes used her intended title, *Ariel*, and published it in 1965. A second version, *Ariel: The Restored Edition, A Facsimile of Plath's Manuscript, Reinstating Her Original Selection and Arrangement*, was published in 2004. For years, Plath scholars had questioned Hughes's choices to remove some of the poems and to shuffle their order. Her other posthumous collections are *Crossing the Water* and *Winter Trees* in 1971. Hughes also published *The Collected Poems* in 1981, which won the 1982 Pulitzer Prize for poetry, and Plath's mother published *Letters Home: Correspondence 1950–1963* in 1975.

Poetic Analysis: "Daddy" and "Lady Lazarus"

Two of Plath's most famous poems are "Daddy" and "Lady Lazarus." In "Daddy," Plath courts controversy by taunting a father figure; the poem's autobiographical details are both accurate and inaccurate. "Daddy" uses intense imagery to portray her father as an abusive Nazi and herself as persecuted like a Jew. It's a puzzling poem, filled with odd rhythms, jarring transitions, and a fierce anger rarely seen in poetry. In "Lady Lazarus," Plath's narrator recalls previous attempts at suicide. It's structured in three-line stanzas, with a subtle occasional rhyme scheme involving the second lines. On the surface, the poem's tone and sound is flippant, an unusual choice given the serious topic.

Humor and Joy

Not all of Plath's poems reflect a tumultuous frame of mind. Some express humor, and even joy. Her poem "You're," is a good example, written when Plath was pregnant with her daughter. A list poem that uses the title as the first line, the poem employs figurative language to playfully describe her growing baby.

The Poet and the Myth

Plath's legacy can be difficult to sort from the almost cult-like status her memory has for certain readers, a fixation that often rests on Plath's suicide at a young age. Although her personal struggles sometimes overshadow her work, she is generally considered to have possessed a great talent, a poet whose body of work merits remembering and reading. Feminists often claim her for their own, although she died before the social movement had fully kicked into gear.

TED HUGHES (1930–1998)

A Force of Nature

Over the course of his long writing career, Ted Hughes developed a reputation as one of England's greatest poets. Hughes was appointed Britain's poet laureate in 1984 and held the post until his death. Early in his career, he was married to poet Sylvia Plath for seven years, until her suicide in 1963.

A YORKSHIRE MAN

Edward James Hughes was born on August 17, 1930, in Mytholmroyd, Yorkshire, to Edith and Billie Hughes. Billie was a carpenter and the family lived in a modest row house with Ted's brother Gerald and sister Olwyn. Mytholmroyd was an industrial village, peppered with textile mills, but surrounded by the desolate Yorkshire countryside. Hughes spent his childhood tramping through that landscape, often following Gerald, his older brother by ten years, as he went on hunting excursions.

He served in the Royal Air Force before attending Pembroke College at Cambridge University. Hughes had intended to study English literature but switched to archaeology and anthropology, finding the subject matter more interesting.

After graduating, Hughes stayed in Cambridge to launch a literary magazine, *Saint Botolph's Review*. The magazine only managed one issue, but it served one unexpected purpose: at the magazine's launch party in 1956, Hughes met his future wife, American poet and Fulbright scholar Sylvia Plath. They married a few months later and stayed in Cambridge for a year while Plath finished her master's degree.

After their marriage, Plath assumed the role of typing Hughes's poems for him. She entered his work into a prestigious first-book contest judged by poets W.H. Auden, Stephen Spender, and Marianne Moore. Hughes's collection, *The Hawk in the Rain*, won and was published to great acclaim in 1957. Hughes's writing style was a departure from the prevailing tastes of the time, which favored quieter poems. Instead, his voice boomed on the page, painting the world in mythic terms and with grand, authoritative diction reminiscent of Shakespeare.

PUBLISHING SUCCESS

In 1960, Hughes published *Lupercal*, which many consider to be his finest work. The poems in *Lupercal* are set in Yorkshire and explore classic Hughes themes of alienation, mythology, and nature. Inspired by his Yorkshire childhood, nature and quite often animals played a central role in Hughes's poems. He portrayed animals with empathy and exquisite detail, rendering them alive on the page, as in 1957's "The Thought-Fox" and 1975's "A March Calf." Hughes's penchant for mythology also ties in with his animal poems; animals frequently take on symbolic characteristics.

Later books include *Wodwo* in 1967, *Crow* in 1970, *Moortown Diary* in 1979, *Selected Poems 1957–1981* in 1982, and *Wolfwatching* in 1989. Hughes also frequently published in literary journals.

Over the years, Hughes wrote more than twenty children's books, including the verse collections *Meet My Folks!* in 1961 and *The Earth-Owl and Other Moon-People* in 1963. His most popular children's book, 1968's *The Iron Man*, was later made into an animated movie. He also was a talented translator who published translations of Ovid, Seneca, and Aeschylus. *Tales from Ovid*, published in 1997, was a critically praised retelling in free verse of twenty-four passages from Ovid's *Metamorphoses*.

Love and Affairs

Hughes's fame is based not only on the quality of his writing, but also on his tabloid-friendly personal life, which involved decades of affairs. Hughes's marriage to Plath fell apart in 1962, when she discovered he was having an affair with one of their tenants, the poet Assia Wevill. Plath left him, taking their two young children, Frieda and Nicholas, with her to a flat in London. She killed herself in early 1963. Tragedy would strike again, six years later, when Wevill killed herself and their four-year-old daughter, Shura.

Frieda Hughes

Frieda Hughes, the daughter of Ted Hughes and Sylvia Plath, followed in her parents' footsteps to become a poet. She has written five collections of poetry, including *Wooroloo* in 1998 and *The Book of Mirrors* in 2009. She said she was in her mid-thirties before she chose to read any of her parents' work, not wanting to be influenced by their styles. Frieda Hughes is also a painter.

Hughes served as executor to Plath's literary estate and edited several volumes of her unpublished work after her death. His treatment of her work, including destroying her last diary and limiting the publication rights to her poems, was met with criticism in literary circles. The wider public could also be unkind: Hughes's name was repeatedly scratched off of Plath's tombstone, and he was sometimes met with anger by outraged fans at his readings. It didn't help that Plath's most celebrated poems, written during the last year of her life, painted him in many cases as a monster who had oppressed her and her talent. Hughes cited protecting Plath's privacy as his reason for not sharing all her work. After years of silence on their marriage, in 1998 he published a series of unsentimental prose poems about their relationship, called *Birthday Letters*.

In October 1998, Hughes was granted the Order of Merit by Queen Elizabeth. Membership is limited to the Queen and twenty-four others. As poet laureate, Hughes had composed poems honoring Queen Elizabeth's sixtieth birthday and the Queen Mother's ninetieth birthday.

Hughes had married Carol Orchard in 1970 and remained married, living together on a farm in Devon, until his death from colon cancer in 1998. He was given a memorial in the Poets' Corner of Westminster Abbey in 2011.

Like many prolific writers, death did not mean the end for Hughes's writing career. Posthumous collections include *Selected Poems 1957–1994* in 2002 and *Collected Poems* in 2003. Hughes was a frequent letter writer during his life. Well-written, lively, and personal, they were compiled into a book, *Letters of Ted Hughes*, in 2007.

THE BEATS

A Generation of Rebels

Say the Beats, and you probably picture men and women in berets and black turtlenecks, smoking cigarettes in a bar, reciting poetry to jazz. The Beats, the Beatniks, whatever you want to call them, came of age in post–World War II America. They tossed out society's rules, and while they were at it, plenty of literature's rules as well.

WHO WERE THE BEATS?

The movement began in New York City's Greenwich Village in the 1940s and had spread to San Francisco by the early 1950s. The Beats were rebelling against the fabric of American culture. They rebelled against the politics of the day. They didn't want to get married, live in a house in the suburbs, and have 2.5 children. They found the pursuit of money amoral and preferred to wear the mantle of poverty. They experimented with hallucinogenic drugs and with sexuality. They rejected their parents' religion. They were bohemians who resisted any kind of restrictions on their lives, believing that freedom would lead to happiness and fulfillment.

As a counterculture, the Beats and their ethos weren't all that well known outside of their enclaves. It took the publication of *Howl and Other Poems* by Allen Ginsberg in 1956 for the Beats to gather widespread public notice. Fellow poet Lawrence Ferlinghetti faced trial on obscenity charges for publishing *Howl* through his City Lights Booksellers and Publishers. The 1957 trial, in which Ferlinghetti was cleared of charges, was covered widely in the media.

Ginsberg was one of a number of writers who gained fame from the movement. Jack Kerouac's 1957 novel *On the Road* defined a generation. William S. Burroughs is best known for his 1959 genre-busting novel *Naked Lunch*. Poets to emerge from the movement included Ginsberg, Ferlinghetti, Gary Snyder, Gregory Corso, Anne Waldman, and Michael McClure.

Why *Beat*?

Jack Kerouac is credited with coming up with the name for the Beat Generation during a conversation between Kerouac and John Clellon Holmes around 1950. *Beat* can mean "worn out and tired," which is how his generation felt in their opposition to mainstream society. It can also be a root for *beatific*, or finding joy in life. The term gained popularity when it was used by Holmes in his November 16, 1952, article in *The New York Times Magazine*, headlined: "This Is the Beat Generation."

To put it mildly, the Beats were not initially welcomed into the established poetry world. There were many critics who deemed their work unworthy of publication, at best, and completely worthless, at worst. Critics didn't know what to make of the unstructured, rambling poems and the angry, sexually explicit lyrics. Others found the new voices exciting and cheered the shift from the staid, traditional-style poems that were popular in the 1950s.

With time, the Beats were grudgingly accepted, then embraced, and are now widely acknowledged as contributing to an important period in America's literary development. Their poems were written to be spoken, sometimes almost sung, out loud. By their joyous embrace of performing poetry in public, they helped revive interest in poetry as performance, a trend that continues today. They pushed cultural limits by writing on previously taboo topics such as homosexuality and drug use, shaking up American sensibilities. Even when faced with censorship, they didn't back down. Collectively, they pushed the boundaries of what defines a poem. Although the Beats as a movement had faded by 1960, their work is still widely read and discussed. *Howl and Other Poems, On the Road*, and *Naked Lunch* have never gone out of print.

Coffeehouse Culture

During the 1950s and 1960s, coffeehouses played a pivotal role in the growing beatnik movement. Small, intimate venues, they provided the perfect inexpensive space for young poets, acoustic folk musicians, and intellectuals to gather for hours of camaraderie. Coffeehouses welcomed individuals who found themselves ostracized elsewhere in society and helped create communities of artists.

ALLEN GINSBERG (1926–1997)

Ginsberg was one of the core members of the Beats; his friendships with Burroughs and Kerouac began while he was a student in the late 1940s at Columbia. Ginsberg initially wrote poetry in the style of Renaissance poets like Sir Thomas Wyatt before rejecting traditional forms in favor of a freewheeling, self-referential style. He claimed Victorian poet William Blake came to him in a vision and inspired him to keep writing.

In 1954, he moved to San Francisco and met Ferlinghetti and Snyder. Ginsberg first shared "Howl" at a Six Gallery reading featuring local poets. "Howl" brought the house down, so to speak. Ginsberg had poured himself into the poem, sharing a lifetime of pain, including repressed homosexuality, and channeled it into verse. Reminiscent in style of Walt Whitman's *Leaves of Grass*, Ginsberg's "Howl" also borrowed from biblical verse like that found in the Psalms. The poem is loosely structured into four parts: first, he lists the pain and destruction society has poured onto his generation; second, he rails against the false values of American culture, embodied as the pagan god Moloch; third, he addresses his friend Carl Solomon and shares, even hopefully, in his madness; and fourth, in a footnote, he finds spirituality and holiness in the world, despite all the depravity.

Ginsberg's other most praised work, *Kaddish*, was published in 1961, and is also written in a prophetic style, reminiscent of the traditional Jewish prayer for the dead. In the poem, Ginsberg mourns the death of his mother, who had suffered from mental illness.

GARY SNYDER (1930–PRESENT)

Snyder was a West Coast poet whose early work aligned with the Beats. Snyder is known for his ecological nature poems, which reflect his Buddhist beliefs. Snyder grew up in Washington and Oregon and interspersed his university education with stints as a logger and a fire watcher. He met the other Beats while living in San Francisco in 1952, where he'd moved to study Asian languages at Berkeley.

Snyder was at Six Gallery, reading his poem "A Berry Feast" the night Ginsberg read "Howl." Unlike some of the Beat poets, Snyder's poetry has consistently garnered praise. His first collection, *Riprap*, published in 1959, established his reputation as a major poet. Snyder moved to Japan in 1956 and spent most of the fifties and sixties living there, or traveling through India, Indonesia, and elsewhere in Asia. His poems have been compared to Ezra Pound's and are precise in their imagery and imaginative in their wordplay. Among his many volumes of poetry, *Turtle Island* in 1974 was granted a Pulitzer Prize. Snyder is fluent in Japanese and Chinese and has translated many poems.

POETRY AS PROTEST

Poetry As an Agent of Change

Poems are just words on a page. But the right words, at the right time, can move people to act. Over the years, especially in the past several centuries, poetry has often served a purpose other than aesthetics. Poetry as protest is a way to bring about change, or, at the very least, call out the *need* for change.

Poetry played a role in some of the biggest societal changes we've seen. It would be impossible to list them all here. Poets have advocated for the rights of women, the disabled, LGBTQs, and minorities. They have protested acts of war and repressive governmental regimes. They have pushed for reforms in schools, workplaces, and places of worship. Poets have fought to retain our wild places and protect animals. They argue for gun control, refugee protections, and healthcare. They protest the patriarchy, the hierarchy, and sometimes, simply, the malarkey, urging us to make sense of the nonsense.

OLD SCHOOL

The Romantics were heavily involved in politics. Percy Bysshe Shelley famously said that "poets are the unacknowledged legislators of the world" in *A Defence of Poetry*. Shelley wrote *The Masque of Anarchy* to protest the 1819 Peterloo Massacre in which a crowd agitating for democratic reform in Manchester, England, was attacked by cavalry, resulting in eleven deaths and 700 injuries. Shelley passionately and eloquently skewers the British ruling class and urges the poor to rise up against them. He advocated for revolution in a lot of his poems, including "Song to the Men of England," which was aimed at downtrodden workers.

In the nineteenth century, some American poets, including Walt Whitman and Henry Wadsworth Longfellow, protested slavery. In 1843, Longfellow wrote *Poems on Slavery* and allowed the New England Anti-Slavery Tract Association to publish them for free in their pamphlets. In "The Warning," a poem quoted often during the Civil War, Longfellow predicts that slavery will destroy American democracy. After slavery was abolished, poets continued to advocate against discrimination. In his 1903 poem "The Haunted Oak," African-American poet Paul Laurence Dunbar protested lynchings by writing movingly from the perspective of an oak tree used by a crowd to lynch an innocent man.

Early twentieth-century poet Carl Sandburg was a radical socialist who used his poems as a rallying cry for the working poor. For his 1916 poem "I Am the People, the Mob," which appeared in his volume *Chicago Poems*, he composed in free verse that feels sonnet-like. Sandburg begins by praising the everyman but turns angry at the willingness of each generation to forget the oppression of those who went before, arguing that change will happen once people learn—and retain—the lessons of the past.

"'Rise like lions after slumber
In unvanquishable number,
Shake your chains to earth like dew
Which in sleep had fallen on you—
Ye are many—they are few.'"

—*The Masque of Anarchy*, Percy Bysshe Shelley

VIETNAM WAR

As we saw in our poetry sections on war, feminism, and African Americans, the 1960s were a period of great social upheaval. Poets were in the forefront. The Vietnam War inspired countless volumes of protest poetry. Prominent poets of the day include Denise Levertov, Allen Ginsberg, Robert Bly, Stephen Dobyns, Gregory Corso, and Philip Levine.

Some poets wrote with empathy about the people in Vietnam who were suffering because of the war. Others wrote angrily about atrocities. Some expressed their profound distress with America itself. Unlike the poems of World War I and II, where poets had been to battle, many of the Vietnam-era poems were inspired by news relayed to the home front in newspaper articles and television reports. Poet Yusef Komunyakaa, who received a Bronze Star for his service as a war correspondent, was an exception. He wrote his 1988 book, *Dien Cai Dau,* from the perspective of the war's African-American soldiers, who fought in disproportionate numbers on the front lines. *Dien Cai Dau* is widely regarded as one of the best books of poetry written about war, praised for its intense imagery and skilled juxtapositions between the perils of war and the comforts of nature.

OTHER VOICES

New voices are always getting added to the mix. In centuries past, most agitators had to be white and privileged themselves in order to advocate for others. In recent decades, poets of all backgrounds have found their voices and now speak out in increasing numbers for themselves. In 2011, the collection *Beauty Is a Verb: The New Poetry of Disability* sought to showcase the rich variety of poems written by poets with disabilities. At ProletarianPoetry.com, British poet and editor Peter Raynard provides a platform for poems by working-class writers.

From the Native American community, Natalie Diaz writes about the struggles of working-class Mojave. In her poem "The Facts of Art," she deftly relates the fraught interactions of Hopi workers with white supervisors who employ them to build a highway through the desert. Layli Long Soldier, a member of the Oglala Sioux Tribe, in her 2017 debut collection, *Whereas,* grapples with treatment of Native Americans. The book includes protest poems such as the title poem, about the virtually unnoticed congressional Native American Apology Resolution, signed by President Obama in 2009 with no Native Americans present. In "38," she uses formal grammar to treat the story of the execution of 38 Dakota men in 1862 with respect, while righteous anger brews just under the poem's restrained surface. Other poets whose work includes protesting white treatment of Native Americans are Simon J. Ortiz, N. Scott Momaday, Leslie Marmon Silko, and Louise Erdrich.

Poet Maggie Smith wrote from her perspective as a mother when she penned "Good Bones," which went viral after forty-nine people were killed by a gunman in a gay nightclub in Orlando, Florida, on June 12, 2016. The poem captures the angst of trying to convince your children the world is a good place when much of it is not. Protest poems have proliferated, shared both online and at protest events, since the election of Donald Trump to the US presidency in 2016. The poems began by protesting his election but have continued in reaction to policies and acts by his administration. Minority voices have been particularly vocal. We'll cover this more in our "Rap and Slam" and "Pushing Poetic Forms" sections.

SEAMUS HEANEY (1939–2013)

A Poet for Ireland

Irish poet Seamus Heaney was born a few months after William Butler Yeats died. Perhaps Yeats passed on the title of most-favored Irish poet to the infant Heaney. Heaney's writing career garnered him both high critical praise, including the 1995 Nobel Prize in Literature, as well as widespread public popularity well beyond Ireland. He did so by writing artful but accessible poems about the Irish people and land.

THE RURAL LIFE

Heaney was born on April 13, 1939, into a Catholic household in Protestant Northern Ireland. His parents were Margaret Kathleen and Patrick Heaney. Heaney grew up in a large family—he was the eldest of nine—on Mossbawn Farm near the village of Bellaghy, between Belfast and Derry. Heaney first attended his local elementary school before transferring as a scholarship student to a boarding school. He attended Queen's University, Belfast, where he majored in English literature and published his first poems in student literary magazines. He graduated in 1961.

After graduation, Heaney taught high school in Belfast for a few years before becoming a lecturer in English at St. Joseph's College of Education. Heaney had met Marie Devlin when they were training to be teachers; they married in 1965. Soon after, he became a lecturer in English at Queen's University, Belfast. Heaney and Devlin, who is also a writer, had three children together.

A Poet Emerges

Heaney's earliest poems tended to be nature poems. His first collections, *Death of a Naturalist* in 1966, followed by *Door into the Dark* in 1969, were similar in theme and style to the work of the poet Ted Hughes, with whom Heaney would later become friends. For both volumes, Heaney drew from his rural upbringing. The work of Robert Frost was also an influence. Frost's descriptions of rural life in New England resonated with Heaney's experiences in rural Ireland. *Death of a Naturalist* burst onto the literary scene, earning Heaney major prizes. These early poems are almost tactile, filled with clear-eyed, pretty, but unsentimental descriptions of daily life in Ireland.

Death of a Naturalist included what may be Heaney's most famous poem, "Digging." In eight irregular stanzas, Heaney vividly depicts his father digging in the garden and his grandfather cutting turf, and compares their labor to the digging he does with a pen, as a writer. The poem doesn't rhyme, but the language heaves and flows with his use of assonance and alliteration. In general, Heaney liked to play with the sound and the cadences of a poem and preferred his rhymes to be just a bit off.

As a minority, Heaney had to navigate an Ireland full of strife. Throughout most of his life, Ireland was embroiled in "the Troubles," the Irish civil unrest between Protestants and Catholics. Heaney began writing about the Troubles in the 1970s, first with his collection *Wintering Out* in 1972 and with *North* in 1975, with a few of the conflict poems also appearing in *Field Work* in 1979. As a poet, Heaney avoided, as much as possible, taking sides. Instead, he found ways to address the conflict by examining it through the lens of history and myth. He also offered moving elegies to personal friends who were killed in the conflicts. With these poems, Heaney was stepping into a fraught position, one with tense feelings all around. It's a testament to his skills as a writer that he didn't alienate all of Ireland, or at least half of it, in the process.

The Academic Life

In 1972, after a year teaching at Berkeley, Heaney quit his job at Queen's University, Belfast, and moved from Northern Ireland to a cottage in County Wicklow in the Irish Republic. While press and critics hypothesized that he went south to take a break from the violence of Belfast, Heaney said he made the move because he needed to make a change to focus on his writing. For four quiet years, he composed poems and worked as a freelance writer. He resumed teaching in 1975, at Carysfort College in Dublin.

Heaney continued to teach at universities through most of his career, often waiting until late at night, when his house was quiet, to work on his poems. During the 1980s, he began teaching at Harvard, eventually being named the Boylston Professor of Rhetoric and Oratory from 1985 to 1996, and would spend four months of each year at Harvard. From 1989 to 1994, he held the prestigious post of Professor of Poetry at Oxford. The position is given to a prominent poet who delivers three lectures a year. Heaney's Oxford lectures were collected and published as *The Redress of Poetry* in 1995.

LONG AND FRUITFUL CAREER

Heaney continued to write and publish throughout the 1980s, 1990s, and 2000s. His reputation only seemed to grow with each collection. His books in the 1980s included *Selected Poems, 1965-1975* in 1980, *Station Island* in 1984, and *The Haw Lantern* in 1987. Heaney's mother had died in 1984. He wrote a touching series of eight sonnets in her memory, called "Clearances," which appeared in *The Haw Lantern*. The sonnets portray an affectionate relationship between the sophisticated son and his rustic mother, grounded in the activities of his mother's life—cooking, laundry, and church.

As he aged, Heaney's style evolved. His poems became less dense with imagery but played more with form. This revised style is evident in *New Selected Poems, 1966–1987*, published in 1990, and a year later, in *Seeing Things*. He continued to write and publish throughout the 1990s and on through to 2010, when his last, and twelfth, collection, *Human Chain*, came out.

Heaney also worked in translation. In 1983, he published *Sweeney Astray: A Version from the Irish*, which translated an Irish lyric poem about an ancient king cursed to be a bird-man. Most notably, his translation of the Anglo-Saxon epic *Beowulf* was an unlikely bestseller in 2000. Heaney managed to pull off rendering the pre-medieval language into a modern voice and was awarded the Whitbread Award.

Happy Birthday

When Seamus Heaney turned seventy in 2009, all of Ireland celebrated with him. The national television station, RTÉ, broadcast more than ten hours of special Heaney-related programming, and museums and schools held special exhibitions and events. As part of the celebrations, it was announced that, in the previous year, Heaney's books had made up two thirds of the living-poet poetry sales in the UK.

On August 30, 2013, Heaney was at a hospital for a scheduled heart surgery but died before the procedure began. His last text to his wife, Marie, was the Latin phrase *Noli timere*, meaning "Do not be afraid." His funeral was attended by members of all of Ireland's political parties, including Ireland's president, and celebrities such as Sting. He is buried in his home village of Bellaghy.

CHARLES SIMIC (1938–PRESENT)

The Immigrant Poet

Charles Simic didn't learn English until he was fifteen years old. Yet he's used his third tongue—his first was Serbo-Croatian, his second, French—to compose some of his adopted language's most celebrated poems. Since the early 1970s, Simic has published more than twenty books of poetry, winning along the way a Pulitzer Prize, a Wallace Stevens Award, and MacArthur, Guggenheim, and National Endowment for the Arts Fellowships. He's also almost singlehandedly introduced the English-speaking world to Serbo-Croatian contemporary poetry. And did we mention, he's also pretty funny?

SURVIVING WAR

A lot of poets claim they had difficult childhoods. Simic grew up in a war zone. Born in Belgrade, Yugoslavia, in 1938, his early years were filled with bombs exploding in his neighborhood. He and other children would scavenge for gunpowder and sell or trade it. At the end of the war, his father made it out to Italy to find work. When Simic was fifteen, his mother managed to get him and his brother to Paris, where she worked as a music teacher. After a year, they joined his father in 1954 in New York, before moving to suburban Chicago. The family had been apart for ten years.

Simic attended high school, hastily learning English to keep up. In Belgrade, he had been a poor student and a self-described troublemaker. In America, though, he applied himself. Within a year or two, he was composing simple poems in English and exchanging them with classmates. He published his first poems in 1959. He entered the University of Chicago, but his education was interrupted in 1961 when the US Army drafted him. He served his two years, then finished his degree at New York University in 1966. To pay the bills while he wrote his poetry, he worked a series of unrelated jobs, painting houses, selling shirts, and so forth, before later becoming a professor. In 1967, he published his first poetry collection, *What the Grass Says*.

A REALIST SURREALIST

Simic's poems are spare in their word choice and precise in their description. He fills them with sharp observations and startling, but apt, comparisons. In just a stanza or two, he can forever change the way you view a fork or a stone, to use two of his poems as examples. In "Fork," Simic points out the eating utensil's similarities to a bird's foot, and draws some surprising conclusions. In "Stone," he imagines himself, happily, living life as a stone, and turns his musings into a contemplation of eternity. Simic plays with how we view reality, calling himself both a realist and a Surrealist.

War, and the hardships it creates, is often present in Simic's work. Bad things happen in his poems but he doesn't beat the drum loudly, shouting at us to protest. Instead, he quietly shows us an image we can't help but be revolted, incensed, or saddened by. Small moments ring loudly: in "The Big War," children play with clay soldiers during the war because, he supposes, the "lead ones they melted into bullets."

Although Simic doesn't make sweeping political statements with his poems, he bears witness to atrocities in a way only a poet can.

Simic has criticized what he views as contemporary poetry's silence on history, questioning why so few events from the recent century are mentioned in verse. Simic as a writer gazes outward—he is rarely at the center of his own poems—a choice that goes against the contemporary current.

Although Simic often portrays the darkness in the world, he is also gifted at finding its absurd humor. His voice is wry and you can sense his amusement in poems such as "Classic Ballroom Dances," when he juxtaposes an image of lovers on a dance floor in a union hall with a charity raffle in the same hall (on Mondays). Elsewhere in his poems, he writes lovingly of food, girlfriends and grandmothers, chickens and jazz—the latter because he is an obsessive early jazz and blues fan.

Prose Poems

Charles Simic's Pulitzer was awarded in 1990 for *The World Doesn't End*, a slim collection of prose poems. Prose poems are hybrids, combining the techniques of poetry—compression, rhythm, imagery—with the line lengths and paragraph structures of prose. Prose poems come in many different sizes and shapes. They date back to nineteenth-century French symbolists rebelling against accepted forms of poetry but have been adapted since then by writers such as James Wright, David Ignatow, and Naomi Shihab Nye.

Simic first taught at California State University, but it was the University of New Hampshire that became home for him: he taught there for more than thirty years. All those years living in the woods, yet he never felt compelled to turn to nature poetry. His landscapes are almost always urban ones, inspired by his childhood in Belgrade and his love of New York.

TRANSLATIONS

Simic is a talented and prolific translator who has spent forty-some years helping bring the work of poets writing in the French and Serbo-Croatian languages into English. Perhaps most notably, he translated and edited *The Horse Has Six Legs: An Anthology of Serbian Poetry* in 1992. The book of contemporary poems by Serbians was released at the peak of the bloody Balkan conflicts.

In 2015, Simic published a collection of his life's essays, pulled together under the title *The Life of Images: Selected Prose*. In the essays, readers get insights into the stories behind the poems. That same year, he also published another poetry collection, *The Lunatic*. His work continues to appear in publications like *The New Yorker*.

Simic was tapped to serve as US poet laureate for a term from 2007 until 2008. During his tenure, he published an anthology of his work, *Sixty Poems*, which provides an appealing introduction to some of his best poems from his many published volumes. Simic's basic style has stayed consistent and recognizable throughout his career. While some critics have considered his lack of evolution a flaw, others find that Simic still has plenty more to say in the way that only he can say it.

LOUISE GLÜCK (1943–PRESENT)

The Cryptic, Quiet Poet

Louise Glück is not a rainbows and puppy dogs kind of poet. Her poems won't fill you to the brim with joy about all the beauty in the world. She's more who you turn to when you want someone to affirm that, yes, life is hard. She won't sugarcoat anything, but at least she will give it to you straight.

For more than fifty years, Glück has been composing lyric poems that thoughtfully peer at the darker aspects of being human. Her efforts have been well praised: she's won just about every poetry prize there is, including the Pulitzer in 1993 and the Bollingen Prize in 2001.

SPARE AND LEAN

Louise Glück was born on April 22, 1943, in New York City. She and her younger sister grew up on Long Island. Her father was a businessman who had wanted to be a writer, and she had a fraught relationship with her mother. As a teen, Glück struggled with anorexia to the point where she needed to drop out of school. She entered into years of psychotherapy, a process she has said helped teach her how to think. She attended Sarah Lawrence College and then Columbia University, where she was mentored by the poet Stanley Kunitz.

She began writing in the 1960s, publishing *Firstborn* in 1968. The collection of first-person poems told from diverse characters' points of view was praised for its originality, its terseness, and its creative use of rhyme. The overall dark and grim tone of the collection pleased some critics but put off others. Her voice was surer when her second collection, *The House on Marshland,* was published seven years later. Glück again used the persona of others to write chilly, formally adept poems, including "Gretel in Darkness," in which Gretel from the fairy tale is haunted by memories of burning the witch.

A Distinctive Style

Glück has published nearly twenty books of poetry. To characterize her style across those many volumes can be a challenge, but there are a few characteristic hallmarks. Glück poems are deceptively simple on the surface. She prefers plain language: she keeps her word choices basic and uses adjectives sparingly. Her lines are typically short—many of her poems look like narrow columns—and even her stanzas tend to be kept in check. Critics often call her style spare and dreamlike. Complexity hides in plain sight: Glück uses extremes, a yin and yang in her poems, to create tension as well as depth.

As for subject matter and approach, she does have certain themes. She covers motherhood (from the perspective of a parent and of a child) as well as marriage (she has been married twice). Her earlier struggles with anorexia find their way into some of her poems, especially when writing about the body. Even when she's writing about herself, her poems often have a universal, mythic feel that turns an exchange between, say, a mother and a daughter into an epic battle for power.

Many of her poems exist in a universe outside Glück's personal experiences, or are at least filtered through the many personas she likes to write from. In *The Wild Iris,* her Pulitzer Prize–winning 1992 collection, Glück writes from the perspective of flowers for a narrative sequence of poems about a garden. While on the surface, it sounds like a nice, light topic—a gardening book!—in Glück's hands, the flowers lead us into ruminations on suffering, death, and burial. It's not all doom and gloom—there are moments of haunting beauty in these poems and profound revelations about the cyclical nature of life.

It's All Greek to Me

One quirk of Glück's work is a reliance on the mythologies of Greece and Rome. The ancient gods and their experiences pop up in her poetry again and again, lending a timelessness to the poems, a sense of history bending in on itself. In 1996's *Meadowlands* she speaks through Odysseus, his abandoned wife Penelope, and their frustrated son, Telemachus, with parallels drawn to the breakup of her own marriage. Or in 2006's *Averno*, Demeter mourns the loss of her daughter Persephone to the lecherous Hades, with parallels drawn to Glück's relationship with her mother.

Glück's fifteenth book, *A Village Life: Poems,* in 2009, was one of her most striking departures. In this volume, the brief lines are replaced by longer, prose-like verse. The effect is more like a novel than a book of poetry. In her most recent collection, *Faithful and Virtuous Night*, published in 2014, she uses a series of imaginative and dreamlike poems to approach the subject of her own mother's death at 101. It won her that year's National Book Award for Poetry.

IN OTHER WORDS

Glück had planned to forge a career in poetry, funded by secretarial jobs, but an unexpected offer from Goddard College in Vermont in the early 1970s set her on a lifetime path of teaching. Glück has also taught at Yale University, where she served as the judge for the Yale Series of Younger Poets from 2003 until 2010, and at Williams College, Columbia University, Boston University, and the University of Iowa.

Glück was named US poet laureate from 2003 to 2004. She had previously served in the capacity of Special Bicentennial Consultant in Poetry with Rita Dove and W.S. Merwin for 1999-2000. A surprised Glück accepted the honor but did so with open trepidation. She is a private poet, someone who loves to write poetry and teach poetry, but doesn't seek out the public. She didn't feel compelled to act as a cheerleader for poetry, a role several of her predecessors eagerly embodied. Her tenure as the poet laureate was a quiet one. Glück's time in the public eye wasn't quite over: in 2015, she was awarded a National Humanities Medal by President Barack Obama.

BILLY COLLINS (1941–PRESENT)

The Playful Poet Laureate

Billy Collins is the kind of poet who doesn't take himself too seriously. This is a man who once published a collection of poems titled *The Trouble with Poetry*. Collins may have a well-developed sense of humor, but he is a serious and well-regarded poet, with a resume featuring a long list of literary and cultural accomplishments. Collins's books break records for poetry sales, his live readings are standing-room-only events, and his name is recognized by university students as well as casual readers who have heard him talking on NPR. He served as the US poet laureate from 2001 to 2003.

A LATE BLOOMER

Born on March 22, 1941, in New York City, Collins was an only child educated at Catholic schools. His mother was a nurse and his father was an electrician who became an insurance broker when Collins was in junior high, prompting a family move from Queens to White Plains, New York. He began writing poems at age ten, inspired by the sight of a sailboat floating on the East River, and continued writing throughout his teens. After earning his bachelor of arts from the College of the Holy Cross in 1963 and a doctorate in Romantic poetry from the University of California, Riverside, in 1971, he began a long career as a professor at Lehman College, City University of New York. Collins was married to architect Diane Olbright from 1978 until their separation in 2006.

Fame as a poet did not come quickly for him. His earlier work was published in *The MidAtlantic Review,* which he co-founded in 1975, and in other small poetry outlets, but it wasn't until 1988 that his first full-length collection of poetry, *The Apple That Astonished Paris,* was published by University of Arkansas Press. He gained widespread attention when his manuscript, *Questions about Angels,* was selected by poet Edward Hirsch in the 1990 National Poetry Series competition, a literary awards program that sponsors the publication of five books of poetry each year.

United States Poets Laureate

Each year since 1937, the Library of Congress in the United States has appointed an official national poet. This poet—known as the "Consultant in Poetry to the Library of Congress" from 1937 to 1986, and as the "Poet Laureate Consultant in Poetry" since 1986—is expected to promote poetry at a national level. Although many poets laureate over the years have composed poems for official government occasions, the post comes with very few official guidelines. In recent years, poets have chosen to organize and lead conferences, visit schools, and lead writing workshops. Fifty-five poets have filled the role, sometimes for terms of more than one year, including Robert Penn Warren, Robert Frost, Maxine Kumin, Rita Dove, and Philip Levine.

Collins has a light touch as a poet, with verses that capture poignant but accessible moments in everyday life. These have helped propel his collections of poetry to the forefront of the American poetry scene. Collins often writes of mundane experiences, whether he is splitting a stack of ash logs or sitting down on a rock bathed in sunlight. His narrative tone is conversational, yet thoughtful, and often leads the reader in surprising directions. He usually writes in free verse, but occasionally uses other forms, including haiku. He is credited with inventing the form paradelle, a parody villanelle, intended as a hoax when he introduced it in the poem "Paradelle for Susan" in 1998 but now used by others as a legitimate form.

Collins is a gregarious and charming speaker, a gift that assisted him as he rose in popularity. After Garrison Keillor interviewed him on NPR's *Prairie Home Companion* in 1998, Collins became one of America's favorite poets. Collins's commercial success as a poet has made waves. He was given a six-figure advance (unheard of in poetry) for a three-book deal when he moved from the University of Pittsburgh Press to Random House in 2001. Several of his nearly one dozen books have made it onto *The New York Times* bestseller lists. His honors include serving as the New York State poet laureate from 2004 to 2006, receiving Fellowships from the Guggenheim Foundation and the National Endowment for the Arts, and being awarded the inaugural Mark Twain Poetry Award for humor in American poetry. In 2016, he was inducted into the American Academy of Arts and Letters.

POETRY 180

As US poet laureate, Collins composed a poem, "The Names," to honor the victims of the September 11 attacks. In September 2002, he read the poem to a special joint session of Congress held in New York City. His role as laureate came with happier tasks as well. Collins's major initiative was Poetry 180, an online anthology of contemporary poems for high school and elementary school teachers. As Collins writes in his intro on the Poetry 180 website, "Poetry can and should be an important part of our daily lives." He selected 180 poems to appeal to high school students and suggests one be read aloud each day: "A great time for the readings would be following the end of daily announcements over the public address system." Collins is a firm believer that poetry should be accessible. By his definition, accessible doesn't mean simple or trite; it refers to poetry that is easy to enter, like a building. Once inside, meaning can be found.

RAP AND SLAM

A Spoken-Word Revolution

Early poetry was exclusively spoken. For illiterate cultures, poetry was a form of entertainment, a pleasure enjoyed communally. Poets passed poems along person-to-person, sharing lyrics that lent themselves, through rhythm and language, to memorization. The invention of the printing press in the fifteenth century ignited a movement toward the printed word, meaning most of us now experience poetry as a silent, solitary activity, eyes scanning pages instead of the faces of the poet and those around us.

Two modern movements help bring poetry directly into our ears: rap and slam. While rap often gets overlooked as a form of poetry, recognition of its value as a literary art form is growing. Slam refers to poetry readings that are held as a contest, with competing poets "slamming" out poems to win over audiences and judges.

RAP

Rap's roots are found in the oral traditions of the African-American population, tracing back through blues and jazz to the field songs of slaves. Rap is particularly influenced, though, by the slavery-era worship tradition of call and response, where a preacher sang a line and the congregation would sing it back. Slavery also left another legacy: slaves used talking drums, an East African invention to allow communications across great distances, to communicate with one another by code. When the drums were outlawed, they continued to use the codes by beating out rhythms on their bodies, a practice called hamboning. Eventually, lyrics were added. In more recent generations, African Americans play a game called the dozens, in which competitors toss insults, often about family members, at each other in rhymed couplets.

Rap is a hybrid of speech and music. Rappers chant lyrics, often rhyming and fast paced, over prerecorded beats and music. As a genre, rap dates to around 1973 when DJ Kool Herc spun records in a new way while his friend Coke La Rock grabbed a microphone and improvised lyrics at a birthday party in the Bronx. Later, groups began to write and memorize lyrics. "The Message," a rap by Bronx-based rappers Grandmaster Flash and the Furious Five, was one of the genre's earliest breakout hits. The lyrics expressed anger, with wit and rhyme, at the rappers' urban existences, hemmed in by poverty, poor education, and lack of opportunities. With rap, teens with few resources found a creative outlet—one that required little money—to communicate their thoughts.

The language is not the kind you'd typically find in an English literature textbook. Rap, especially in its first two decades, was rife with expletives and sexually explicit lyrics. It's rarely included in poetry textbooks and other resource books. Yet, there are parallels to be made between rap and the African-American protest poetry from the 1960s, which called out, honestly and explicitly, the difficulties of being black in America. There are also parallels to the poetic style of the Harlem Renaissance. Just as African-American poets in the 1920s drew from jazz and blues to shape their lyrics, rappers use the same influences, as well as gospel, funk, and reggae, to craft rap. Their artistic efforts have proven so successful that they have moved well beyond audiences in the original South Bronx neighborhoods to throughout the world. Poet Nikki Giovanni has been a proponent of considering rap as poetry, praising its ability to share the stories of everyday people.

SLAM

In 1984, poet and construction worker Marc Smith began hosting a staged event for poets weekly at the Get Me High jazz club in Chicago. Smith envisioned a livelier event than most open mics. He matched poets against each other and encouraged audience participation. The idea took off, and in 1986, Smith moved the event to Green Mill cocktail lounge. He dubbed the weekly event the Uptown Poetry Cabaret. (The slam is ongoing, more than twenty years later.)

The concept soon spread well beyond Chicago. Poetry slams began popping up in bars, coffee shops, and libraries in cities across the US, then throughout Europe. Rules were established: poets have three minutes to perform original poems without props, costumes, or instruments. Five judges, sometimes picked randomly from the audience, give scores based on a 1–10 scale; the highest and lowest scores are dropped. Audiences are encouraged to snap fingers, clap, or call out praise or insults. Prizes at the end of the night may be the money collected at the door from attendees.

The National Poetry Slam began in San Francisco in 1990 with a host city team, a Chicago team, and one poet from New York. The weeklong competition now annually attracts more than seventy national and international teams, consisting of three to five people, to a different host city each summer. An Individual World Poetry Slam (IWPS) also takes place annually. Poetry Slam Inc., a nonprofit founded in 1997, organizes the competitions and certifies local slam groups. Other groups also organize slams and competitions, including the Brave New Voices International Youth Poetry Slam Festival for teens, which celebrated its twentieth year in 2017.

Def Poetry Jam

From 2002–2007, HBO aired *Russell Simmons Presents Def Poetry*, a series hosted by Mos Def. National Poetry Slam champions were some of the performers on the show, as well as established poets such as Nikki Giovanni, Amiri Baraka, and Sonia Sanchez. *Def Poetry Jam* also ran on Broadway from November 2002 until May 2003 and won a 2003 Tony Award for Best Special Theatrical Event.

At a slam, any kind of poetry can be performed. There are no limits on subject or style, although poets who compose their work with an ear toward how the poem will be heard are more likely to do well. The informal and inclusive atmosphere welcomes all ages, ethnicities, nationalities, sexes, religions, and identities. Slams are *YouTube*- and social media–friendly events and have helped launch the careers of some poets. Poet Patricia Smith won the IWPS four times and counts among her other honors a Guggenheim Fellowship and two Pushcart Prizes. Danez Smith, the author of *Don't Call Us Dead*, a finalist for the 2017 National Book Award, was a 2011 IWPS finalist.

RUPI KAUR (1992–PRESENT)

The Instapoet

Rupi Kaur is an artist and poet who came to fame through a very modern means: *Instagram.* As a teen, she began posting sketches, photographs, and poems on social media platforms. She's now published two bestselling books of poetry and amassed more than 2.6 million followers on *Instagram,* nearly 483,000 on *Facebook* and almost 200,000 on *Twitter.* As a poet, she's attained a level of celebrity status usually granted to musicians or actors.

INSTAGRAM FAMOUS

Kaur was born in Punjab, India, in 1992. When she was three, she emigrated with her Sikh parents to Ontario, Canada, where her father found work as a truck driver. She has three younger siblings. As a kid, Kaur enjoyed writing and drawing, encouraged by her mother. In her teens, she began blogging and posting to *Tumblr,* publishing under her own name by 2013.

Instagram, however, proved to be the perfect match for her mix of art and poetry. She grew a steady, if not overwhelming, following for the brief poems she published there, usually illustrated by one of Kaur's doodle-like line drawings. Kaur was encouraged by her online audience to compile the poems into a book. Rather than try to go the route of a traditional publisher, Kaur decided to put the book together on her own. Using *Amazon*'s CreateSpace, she self-published her first collection of poems and sketches, *Milk and Honey,* in 2014.

Her ascent to Internet celebrity was unrelated to her poetry. In early 2015, as a student at the University of Waterloo, Kaur published an *Instagram* photograph of herself lying on a bed, wearing sweatpants with a stain from a menstrual blood leak. She'd had her sister take the image for her, as part of a class assignment on breaking taboos. *Instagram* removed the photo, prompting Kaur to accuse them—emphatically—on *Tumblr* and *Facebook* of misogyny. Her *Facebook* post went viral and *Instagram* responded by reposting the photograph. The kerfuffle raised Kaur's online profile significantly, and she became an Internet spokesperson for feminism.

Like Rupi Kaur?

A quick Internet search shows numerous blogs recommending poets to try if you enjoy Kaur's work. Poets currently writing include: Aimee Nezhukumatathil, Kim Addonizio, Patricia Smith, and Ilya Kaminsky. Looking for classics? Try Lucille Clifton, Maya Angelou, Sylvia Plath, and Anne Sexton.

As Kaur's name ricocheted around the Internet, sales for *Milk and Honey* skyrocketed, attracting the attention of Andrews McMeel Publishing. They approached Kaur about reissuing the book. Since it was released in 2015, it has sold an unprecedented more than 2.5 million copies. Its success was startling, especially for a new poet: the book remained on *The New York Times* bestseller list for paperback trade fiction for nine weeks in a row.

Her second collection, *The Sun and Her Flowers*, was published in October 2017. Its sales have also been strong: it ranked Number 1 on the *Publishers Weekly* trade paperback list for its first ten weeks. Kaur's promotions for the second collection included an exclusive

Entertainment Weekly preview of the cover as well as a *Rolling Stone* profile piece. She launched *The Sun and Her Flowers* with a sold-out event at the Tribeca Performing Arts Center and has toured for the book in the United States and abroad. Her readings are upbeat affairs accompanied by pop music, the seats packed with her young female admirers. They aren't the quiet wine and cheese affairs held at bookstores or on university campuses where we normally find poets.

POEMS FOR A NEW GENERATION

That's the fame piece. Now, what about the poetry?

Kaur's poems are brief and to the point, sometimes only a sentence or two, perfect for framing within an *Instagram* square. Her themes tend to revolve around her experiences as a young woman. She writes about relationships, heartbreaks, self-care, nature, friendships, and quite often, about female empowerment. The poems are emotional and heartfelt, which wins her both admirers and detractors. She eschews capitalization and all punctuation except periods. In some interviews, she has said the choice is a nod to her parents' native language of Punjabi.

It can be difficult to be a woman writing online. The medium is notorious as a venue for cruelty. Parody poems of Kaur's work abound, taking on lives of their own in mock *Twitter* and *Instagram* accounts. Her taunters take nearly any sentence, insert random breaks, and throw a "—Rupi Kaur" at the bottom, turning nonsense into "poetry." An entire book of such poems, called *Milk and Vine*, has become a bestseller on *Amazon*. Her work can feel familiar in its generalities, a trait that may be responsible for the accusation of plagiarism she occasionally receives from other online poets.

As a Southeast Asian Sikh, Kaur is a minority in the world of English-language poetry. In some of her poems, she has adopted an "I" that is not her own, writing about violence against women of color that she has not personally experienced. Although some applaud her efforts to bring those stories to a wider audience, others have criticized her for sharing experiences that they argue aren't hers to claim. Kaur asserts that the abuse is inherent in her ancestry, that women carry it with them from generation to generation. Perhaps in answer to her critics, her second book delves into her experiences as the child of immigrants and explores her race more clearly than in her earlier work.

Kaur's poetry resonates with a large demographic who find she articulates feelings and emotions they have trouble articulating for themselves. While critics throw words such as trite, angsty, and vapid around when describing her work, many also acknowledge that Kaur's poetry is encouraging a new generation to read poetry. Whether legions of those new readers will make the leap to discover other poets, or will remain firmly in the Kaur bubble, remains to be seen.

Other Instapoets

Rupi Kaur is not alone in finding fame, and a publishing deal, as an Internet poet. She belongs to a rapidly growing number of poets who collectively have been dubbed "Instapoets." Poets Lang Leav, Robert M. Drake, Nayyirah Waheed, and Tyler Knott Gregson are among those whose poetry has gone viral online and then sold well off-line.

The term *Instapoet* annoys some of the writers to whom it has been applied because it says little more than where the poems were originally published, lumping writers of widely different styles into a single group. By using online platforms to reach readers directly, without having to go through traditional publishing gatekeepers, the trend has helped to bring the work of young, diverse poets to wider audiences.

WRITING POETRY

Finding Your Own Voice

There's no one-size-fits-all approach to writing poetry. As we've seen in this book, the voice of each poet is unique, and even fluid, shifting subtly or dramatically from poem to poem. To write a good poem, a poet relies not only on inspiration but skill built by hard work. We can give you a few tips for how to put in the work it takes to craft poems with artistic merit and where to look for inspiration. Consider this section a jumping-off point for your own creativity.

PREPARING TO WRITE

We're talking about more than just sharpening pencils or turning off alerts to your *Facebook* and *Instagram* accounts. Here are a few ideas about what to do *before* you sit down to face that blank page.

Read, Read, Read

Congratulations! You're already off to a good start because you're reading this book. Now, take our advice from way back in the introduction and get your hands on some poems. Read them online, subscribe to poetry journals, or grab an old-fashioned book, but get familiar with a wide variety of poetry. Anthologies are a good starting point. Once you find a few poets you enjoy, dive in deeper and get a feel for their body of work. When you find poems you like, spend some time with them. Figure out what the appeal is and you'll have a better shot later of creating similarly appealing poems.

Books on writing also deserve your attention. Not only will they offer advice for how to write good poems, they'll give you a vocabulary to talk about your writing. Check to see if any of your favorite poets have published a book about writing.

While we're advocating for reading, don't forget to keep up on news and maybe even brush up on history or literature or science. Good poems are always about more than just feelings. Poets who create dense, sophisticated poetry often do so by drawing from knowledge gained from other sources. We're not being snobs here. If celebrity news is your thing, and you'd like to write poems about the entertainment world, then catching up with the Kardashians is a good use of your time. Find your niche and dig deep.

Keep a Journal

A journal will help you hone your observational skills. It provides a low-key, no-pressure kind of place to jot down ideas or descriptions. You can write poems here, but don't get too attached to them. Think of it as a place to deposit the seeds you will later grow into poems.

ON WRITING

Ready to write? Great. Where to start?

Get Inspired

If you're stuck for ideas, thumb through that journal you've been keeping and see if you feel like planting any of the seeds you threw in there. There's no lack of places to look for inspiration and no limits to the number of writing prompts you can find online. Stay loose as you start to write and remember you'll be able to make changes later.

Always Revise

- The clarity of language found in poems takes effort. Once you've finished a poem, step away. Get some distance before returning to it again. Flaws will be clearer later.
- On your next go, listen as you read it out loud. Mark places where the words trip you or where the rhythm feels off. Are there ways to make the language flow better? Are the line breaks working?
- Did any clichés sneak in? Can the language be condensed? Can you use any similes or metaphors? Are there words that could be replaced, either to make the poem's meaning clearer or sound better? Does the poem have the tone you want?
- Resist the urge to conclude with a stanza summing up the poem. A little ambiguity goes a long way.

FIND A COMMUNITY

While it's romantic to think of a poet sitting alone in a drafty garret, scribbling madly away in a notebook, the reality is that poets don't need to work in isolation. Finding other poets to interact with can play a vital role in helping you grow as a poet.

Attend a Reading

Bookstores, libraries, and universities host poets regularly for readings. With a little research, you can track down what events are happening near you, maybe even to find a poetry slam. Hearing poets read their own work brings their poetry to life and can help inspire you to keep plugging away at your own work. (You also might find some kindred spirits in the audience.)

Join a Writing Group

Participating in a writing group can help develop your critical reading skills and can provide much-needed feedback on your own work-in-progress. Many writers also find that the pressure of getting poems ready for the next group gathering motivates them to write and revise.

Take a Class

Check with your local library or parks and recreation department for listings of adult education or enrichment courses. Intended for personal development, these classes can offer a gentle, grade-free environment to develop your writing. Ready to take the next step? Many universities and community colleges also offer writing classes, which may be available to nonmatriculated students for a tuition fee, or in the case of senior citizens, sometimes for free if you audit.

Earn an MFA

Creative writing programs offering a master's of fine arts have proliferated in the last several decades. There may be one offered at a nearby institution or you could consider enrolling in a nonresident or online program. Honing your craft for two or three years in a poetry track puts you on a serious path toward poet-hood. Graduates have a body of work to publish, a credential to teach, and a wealth of knowledge they can draw from throughout the rest of their writing lives.

GETTING PUBLISHED

Getting "published" can mean a lot of things these days. It may mean posting your poems yourself to a blog or on social media, or having a poem accepted by a literary journal, either online or in print. For more established poets, publishing a chapbook of selected poems through a small press or university press is a big step. Others take the plunge themselves and publish their own book. A few, very rare, commercially successful poets publish through the major publishing houses.

If you want to pursue external publishing, be patient. Know that even very good poems may be rejected dozens of times. Keep trying and keep experimenting. That unique voice—your voice—is waiting to be discovered.

PUSHING POETIC FORMS

The Future of Poetry

As we've seen in these pages, poetry is an ever-evolving art form. Although some universals stay the same—poets of every generation have tackled the topics of love and death—other aspects of poetry radically change. Each generation tries to push poetry to reflect their own creative processes, not to mention cultural, political, and aesthetic sensibilities. The launch of social media in the past twenty years has had a profound effect on how poetry is made and shared. While not all new poetry forms are related to the Internet, it is easily the biggest game-changing development for writers in the modern world.

TWITTER

Poets have frequently written poems using constrictions dictated by form: a haiku must have three lines, a limerick five, and a sonnet fourteen lines. So when *Twitter* came along, with its character restrictions, it's not shocking that some poets responded: challenge accepted. *Twitter* poems have even inspired their own names: twihaiku or micropoetry. Originally, tweets could only contain 140 characters. The limit has now stretched to 280 characters, but the format is still succinct.

British poet Brian Bilston accumulated 52,000 followers by posting his quirky, humorous poems on *Twitter*. Dubbed *Twitter*'s poet laureate by the UK media, Bilston's poems range from visual poems to political and social commentary, almost always with a satirical bent. Although he sometimes uses the platform to show images of longer poems, he still frequently shares poems that fit into a single tweet.

Established poets have also found the platform useful. Popular British dub poet Benjamin Zephaniah, who published his first collection of poetry in 1980, occasionally tweets verse from poems he is working on. Faber Prize–winning poet George Szirtes also likes to post new poems to his *Twitter* feed. Poets and poetry lovers use the site to share their own and other poets' work, sometimes as attached images when the poems are too long for a single tweet.

Twitter allows for poetry, both new and newly relevant, to be shared immediately in response to news and events. After the 2016 US election, poetry site Poets.org saw a huge increase in the number of people tweeting out classic activist poems, including Maya Angelou's "Still I Rise" and Langston Hughes's "Let America Be America Again." While Black Lives Matter poems may not have made it into books yet, they are everywhere on *Twitter*. Danez Smith's "the bullet was a girl," and "what the dead know by heart" by Donte Collins are frequently circulated online.

YOUTUBE

As a visual medium, *YouTube* lends itself both to spoken-word poets and to video poems. The site makes it easy for fans to see their favorite poets recite, or rather, perform, their poems. Two of the biggest names are British poets Kate Tempest and Hollie McNish, both winners of the Ted Hughes Award for New Work in Poetry, who have amassed huge online followings for their bombastic styles of poetry. Tempest is a rapper, novelist, and spoken-word poet in her early thirties, whose work draws from classic poets such as William Blake and T.S. Eliot as well as vintage rap. She portrays a rough-on-the-edges London life in mythic terms. Hollie McNish writes in an informal, almost chatty style about daily struggles. Her poem about breastfeeding, "Embarrassed," went viral. You can watch McNish read it on a stage, or, music-video style, see it recited in different scenes showing other mothers and the reactions they receive when nursing in public.

American Sign Language

Poets who compose using American Sign Language have found *YouTube* to be a great vehicle to share and promote their work. Some of the videos include subtitles or voice-overs for viewers who can't read ASL. Deaf poets also sometimes perform poems from other poets, including Neil Gaiman, Emily Dickinson, and Edgar Allan Poe, providing a new way of "reading" their work.

Video poems, sometimes called cinepoetry, are growing in popularity. Poets are exploring the ways that visual images, sound, and music can enhance their words. There isn't a set format—poets may collaborate with musicians or choose to recite alone—but the medium offers a visual counterpoint to the poet's text. Poet and hip-hop artist Slim da Reazon partnered with singer Audra Bryant for the music video for his poem "Beautiful You," which includes scenes with Reazon performing his poem in an elegant house. Vanessa Angélica Villarreal uses a documentary style for the video for her poem, "Estrellada." Villarreal recites the poem over a quiet instrumental track while showing footage of clouds, rooms in her house, and family photographs. Filmmaker Gabe Rubin takes another approach in a video with poet Charles Bernstein, filming him reading his poem "On Election Day" at locations throughout Brooklyn. Background noise from the locations isn't filtered out and, occasionally, a voice from off camera joins Bernstein for lines.

IS POETRY TOO POPULAR?

Some posit that the Internet gives some poets an audience they don't deserve, that the rush to share-and-be-shared only ends up perpetuating poor poems. With no editors or gatekeepers, anything goes. *PN Review*, a prominent British poetry journal, published a scathing article by critic Rebecca Watts in February 2018 that took aim at poets with Internet fame, including Tempest, McNish, and Rupi Kaur. Watts lamented what she views as commercially driven poetry—popular, but ultimately not art.

Art is subjective. For every Watts who hates the new Internet-friendly poems, there are counterparts lining up to praise the accessibility and honesty of the new breed of poet. No poet—or poetic movement—has ever been greeted enthusiastically by all. Even Byron, Keats, Whitman, Pound, Hughes, and Plath were derided in their day. What is true is that poetry, whether everyone likes it or not, is moving away from an elite mountaintop straight down into our pockets. Today's readers live in a golden age of information, carrying complete libraries in our phones, tablets, and laptops. Modern tech allows us to enjoy poets from all eras, anytime, anywhere.

INDEX